Grade
2

flag

Second Grade
Fundamentals

Brighter Child®
An imprint of Carson-Dellosa Publishing LLC
P.O. Box 35665
Greensboro, NC 27425 USA

ISBN 978-1-60996-829-8

RB-152127784

Table of Contents

Table of Contents

© Rainbow Bridge Publishing

Recommended Reading List

Adler, David A.
Cam Jansen: The Mystery of the Dinosaur Bones

Ahlberg, Allan
The Runaway Dinner

Armstrong, Jennifer
Sunshine, Moonshine

Arnold, Tedd
The Twin Princes

Babbitt, Natalie
Jack Plank Tells Tales

Barracca, Debra & Sal
The Adventures of Taxi Dog

Bemelmans, Ludwig
Madeline

Bishop, Claire Huchet
The Five Chinese Brothers

Bond, Michael
Paddington Bear series

Brenner, Barbara
Wagon Wheels

Brown, Margaret Wise
The Important Book

Browne, Anthony
Voices in the Park

Bunting, Eve
A Day's Work

Burton, Virginia Lee
Mike Mulligan and His Steam Shovel

Charlip, Remy
Fortunately

Christelow, Eileen
What Do Authors Do?

Christopher, Matt
The Dog That Pitched a No-Hitter

Coerr, Eleanor
Chang's Paper Pony

Collins, Pat Lowery
I Am an Artist

Coxe, Molly
Big Egg

Coy, John
Night Driving

Cushman, Doug
Aunt Eater Loves a Mystery

Delton, Judy
Pee Wee Scouts series

Dooley, Norah
Everybody Cooks Rice

Falconer, Ian
Olivia

Fox, Mem
Wilfrid Gordon McDonald Partridge

Freeman, Don
Corduroy

Friend, Catherine
The Perfect Nest

Garland, Sherry
The Lotus Seed

Gray, Libba Moore
My Mama Had a Dancing Heart

Grogan, John
Bad Dog, Marley!

Hartman, Bob
The Wolf Who Cried Boy

Heard, Georgia
Creatures of Earth, Sea, and Sky: Poems

Heide, Florence Parry
The Shrinking of Treehorn

Henkes, Kevin
Lilly's Big Day

Herman, Gail
The Lion and the Mouse

Hoff, Syd
The Horse in Harry's Room

Holabird, Katharine
Angelina Ballerina

Jenkins, Steve
Dogs and Cats

Johnson, Stephen T.
My Little Yellow Taxi

Kann, Elizabeth
Victoria Pinkalicious

Keats, Ezra Jack
A Letter to Amy

Kelley, Ellen A.
Buckamoo Girls

Kessler, Leonard
Here Comes the Strikeout

Kimmel, Eric A.
The Chanukkah Guest

Komaiko, Leah
Annie Bananie

Recommended Reading List

Kuskin, Karla
Soap Soup: And Other Verses

LaRochelle, David
The End

Leaf, Munro
The Story of Ferdinand

Lobel, Arnold
Frog and Toad Are Friends

Long, Melinda
How I Became a Pirate

Lowry, Lois
Gooney the Fabulous

MacLachlan, Patricia
All the Places to Love

Mayer, Mercer
Just Me and My Dad

McCloskey, Robert
Blueberries for Sal

McKissack, Patricia C.
The Honest-to-Goodness Truth

Melling, David
The Scallywags

Mosel, Arlene
Tikki Tikki Tembo

Mozelle, Shirley
Zack's Alligator

Nixon, Joan Lowery
If You Were a Writer

Numeroff, Laura Joffe
If You Give a Mouse a Cookie

O'Connor, Jane
Fancy Nancy

Parish, Peggy
Amelia Bedelia

Park, Frances & Ginger
The Royal Bee

Pennypacker, Sara
The Talented Clementine

Piper, Watty
The Little Engine That Could

Platt, Kin
Big Max

Rathmann, Peggy
Ruby the Copycat

Regan, Dana
Monkey See, Monkey Do

Rey, H. A. & Margret
The Complete Adventures of Curious George

Rylant, Cynthia
Night in the Country

Schotter, Roni
Nothing Ever Happens on 90th Street

Sharmat, Mitchell
Gregory, the Terrible Eater

S..... .in, Shel
The Giving Tree

Small, David
Imogene's Antlers

Steig, William
Caleb & Kate

Stock, Catherine
Where Are You Going, Manyoni?

Teague, Mark
The Secret Shortcut

Thomas, Shelley Moore
Good Night, Good Knight

Thompson, Kay
Eloise

Walton, Rick
Bullfrog Pops!

Ward, Lynd
The Biggest Bear

Wiesner, David
Free Fall

Williams, Vera B.
A Chair for My Mother

Ziefert, Harriet
A New Coat for Anna

Zion, Gene
Harry by the Sea

Zolotow, Charlotte
If You Listen

Initial Consonants

Say the name of each picture. Write the letter for the beginning sound.

1.

_ o g

2.

_ o u s e

3.

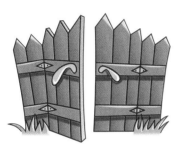

_ a t e

4.

_ e n t

5.

_ i k e

6.

_ e e r

Final Consonants

Say the name of each picture. Write the letter for the ending sound.

1.

c o r

2.

b e

3.

b o o

4.

c a

5.

l e a

6.

d r u

Medial Consonants

Say the name of each picture. Circle the letter for the middle sound.

1.

   r
   n
   b
   c

2.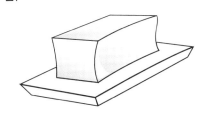

   s
   r
   b
   t

3.

   p
   l
   g
   w

4.

   o
   p
   l
   f

5.

   r
   l
   d
   c

6.

   r
   s
   p
   z

7.

   c
   r
   t
   k

8.

   n
   t
   b
   d

Short Vowels: A

Draw a line through the three rhyming words in each group. Lines can go across, up, down, or diagonally.

1.	pat	mat	fat	2. ram	wag	bag
	ram	cab	bag	rag	ham	fan
	lamp	tab	tan	rat	Pat	Pam

3.	lamp	sag	can	4. ran	ax	tan
	tap	map	cap	sad	wax	lap
	tag	bag	cat	pan	tax	nap

5.	hat	lamp	Jan	6. dad	Sam	gas
	ant	yam	jam	man	pad	can
	bad	mad	had	at	an	lad

Short Vowels: E

Help Deb get Pepper to the vet. Look at the Word Bank. Write the name of each picture on the line.

Word Bank

jet
bed
vet
web
tent

Short Vowels: I

Choose one word for each sentence to make a silly story. Circle the word. Then, write it on the line.

_____

— — — — — — — — — — — — —

1. Mom let us _____ in the sink.

bib
rip
fish

_____
_____

— — — — — — — — — — — — —

2. We fill the _____ with water.

fill
sink
fish

_____
_____

— — — — — — — — — — — — —

3. Kim put in _____ fish.

six
fit
hill

_____
_____

— — — — — — — — — — — — —

4. Look, they like to _____ .

wish
swim
will

_____
_____

— — — — — — — — — — — — —

5. I _____ I was a fish.

fig
wish
lick

_____

Short Vowels: O

Underline the words with the short *o* sound.

1. You can eat a hot dog.

2. A frog lives in a pond.

3. Mom can sit on a log.

4. The rock is hot.

5. Drink the last drop in the pot.

6. Tom has a lot of socks.

7. You can lock the box.

8. The doll has a mop.

9. The fox loves his new box.

10. Bobby likes to collect rocks.

Short Vowels: U

Choose one word for each sentence to make a silly story. Circle the word. Then, write it on the line.

sub
cub
1. Today, I rode on a _____. skunk

tub
jug
2. Then, I took a nap in the _____. mud

bugs
gum
3. For lunch, I ate _____. nuts

bus
slug
4. A _____ ran off with my mug. duck

rug
bun
5. So, I sat in a _____ in the sun. cup

Long Vowels: A

Look at the Word Bank. Write the name of each picture on the line. Then, circle the word in the puzzle. Words can go across, up, down, or diagonally.

1.

_____

- - - - - - - - - -

_____

Word Bank

plate

cake

pail

rain

2.

_____

- - - - - - - - - -

_____

3.

_____

- - - - - - - - - -

_____

4.

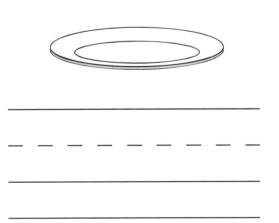

_____

- - - - - - - - - -

_____

d	c	a	r	f	r	p	w
p	c	p	s	r	t	a	k
z	l	l	r	c	e	i	a
c	a	a	s	a	k	l	i
k	g	r	t	w	a	x	g
c	w	r	a	e	c	i	u
a	a	m	t	i	n	l	u
m	y	l	b	f	n	v	v

14

Long Vowels: E

Use the words in the Word Bank to finish the story. Write the words on the lines. Then, circle the words in the puzzle. Words can go across, up, down, or diagonally.

Word Bank					
sea	feet	beak	week	eat	tree

_____

– – – – – – – –

I had a dream last _____ . I saw a seal in the

_____   _____

– – – – – – –   – – – – – – – –

_____ . It had a _____ for a nose

_____   _____

– – – – – – –   – – – – – – –

and six _____ . It tried to _____ a

_____   _____

– – – – – – –

leaf on a _____ .

_____

```
f  e  e  t  q  m  y  e
g  z  m  k  i  f  u  d
o  k  z  w  e  e  k  w
q  t  r  e  e  a  b  w
u  s  e  a  s  t  t  i
b  e  a  k  i  c  w  a
d  t  x  o  n  h  s  l
```

Long Vowels: I

Ty and Mike are going to do something. Choose a word from the Word Bank that rhymes with the bold word to complete each sentence. Then, write it on the line.

Word Bank

bike	mile	line	side	fly

---

1. Get the one I **like**, the big red _____.

2. Hurry, **Ty**, we have to _____.

3. I have **mine**, so get in _____.

4. Now, when we **ride**, stay on my _____.

5. It takes a **while** to go a _____.

On a separate sheet of paper, write about what you think Ty and Mike are doing. Use some of the long _i_ words from the Word Bank.

Long Vowels: O

Circle the word that solves each riddle. Then, write it on the line.

1. A car can drive on it.

   _____

   hope
   road
   rope

2. We wash our hands with it.

   _____

   toe
   rose
   soap

3. It is green and likes to hop.

   _____

   boat
   toad
   goat

4. You put it on when it is cold.

   _____

   moat
   coat
   nose

5. You write it to tell something.

   _____

   note
   bone
   soak

6. A dog can chew on it.

   _____

   bone
   coat
   soap

Long Vowels: U

Look at the Word Bank. Choose a word that tells about each picture. Then, write the word on the line.

Word Bank			
music	tube	flute	bugle

1.

_____

_ _ _ _ _ _ _ _ _ _ _ _ _ _

_____

2.

_____

_ _ _ _ _ _ _ _ _ _ _ _ _ _

_____

3.

_____

_ _ _ _ _ _ _ _ _ _ _ _ _ _

_____

4.

_____

_ _ _ _ _ _ _ _ _ _ _ _ _ _

_____

Compound Words

A compound word is two words put together to make one new word. Help Robin Hood make new words. Draw a line from one word to another to make a compound word.

1.	base	bow
2.	pea	cake
3.	oat	time
4.	cup	ball
5.	rain	meal
6.	bed	nut

Write the compound words on the lines.

7. _____

8. _____

9. _____

10. _____

11. _____

12. _____

Compound Crossword

Write the correct word from the Word Bank on the line below each clue.

Word Bank			
pancake	sailboat	backpack	sandbox
mailbox	anthill	raincoat	popcorn

Across

2. A hill for ants

_ _ _ _ _ _ _

3. Corn you can pop

_ _ _ _ _ _ _

6. A flat cake cooked in a pan

_ _ _ _ _ _ _

7. A box to hold mail

_ _ _ _ _ _ _

8. A box full of sand

_ _ _ _ _ _ _

Down

1. A pack for your back

_ _ _ _ _ _ _ _

4. A coat to wear in the rain

_ _ _ _ _ _ _

5. A boat with a sail

_ _ _ _ _ _ _ _

Compound Crossword

Use the answers (page 20) to complete the crossword puzzle.

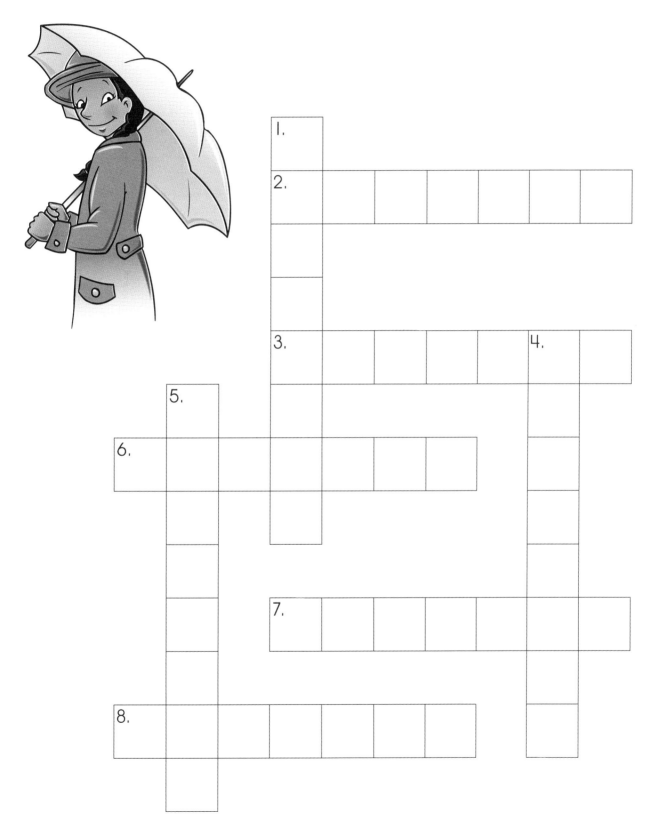

Two-Syllable Words

If two vowels are heard when a word is spoken, the word has two syllables. Say the words in each box. Circle the vowels you hear. Write each two-syllable word on the line below its box.

1.
kite	got
bed	open

_____

- - - - - - - - -

_____

2.
tree	boxes
cake	sea

_____

- - - - - - - - -

_____

3.
dime	note
inside	toad

_____

- - - - - - - - -

_____

4.
sand	mail
take	puppet

_____

- - - - - - - - -

_____

5.
mitten	best
tent	socks

_____

- - - - - - - - -

_____

6.
egg	feet
road	wagons

_____

- - - - - - - - -

_____

Words Ending in -LE

Choose the word from the Word Bank that solves each riddle. Then, write it on the line.

> ## Word Bank
> whistle   puddle   giggle   candle   apple   bubble

1. One of these was lit for your first birthday. _____

2. This makes a sound when you blow it. _____

3. You get wet when you jump in this. _____

4. You do this when someone tickles you. _____

5. This fruit makes a tasty snack. _____

6. You can blow this with gum. _____

Words Ending in -LE

On each line, write the number of the sentence that tells about the picture.

A. Look, those people are on the table.

B. How did that turtle get in the bottle?

C. That apple will fall on the candle.

D. Can all eagles blow a bubble?

1.

_____
- - - - - - - - - - -
_____
_____

2.

_____
- - - - - - - - - - -
_____
_____

3.

_____
- - - - - - - - - - -
_____
_____

4.

_____
- - - - - - - - - - -
_____
_____

Hard and Soft C

When *c* is followed by *e* or *i*, the *c* makes a soft sound as in *circle*. When *c* is followed by *o* or *a*, the *c* makes a hard sound as in *cow*.

Choose the correct word from the Word Bank to complete each sentence. Write it on the line. Then, circle each hard *c* word in red. Circle each soft *c* word in yellow.

Word Bank			
city	cent	cat	cell

1. We took a cab into the _____.

2. Two mice stare at the _____.

3. Come here and answer your _____ phone.

4. Can't you loan me one _____?

Hard and Soft C

Read the list of *c* words in the Word Bank. Write the hard *c* words on the lines under Carrie. Write the soft *c* words on the lines under Cecil.

Carrie

_____

_____

_____

_____

_____

_____

Word Bank

circle

carrot

cereal

cone

cane

center

cellar

camel

celery

case

Cecil

_____

_____

_____

_____

_____

_____

Hard and Soft G

When *g* is followed by *e*, *i*, or *y* the *g* makes a soft sound as in *genie*. When *g* is followed by *o*, *a*, or *u* the *g* makes a hard sound as in *go*.

Read each word. Fill in the correct circle to show if the *g* makes a hard or soft sound.

1. gate
    - ○ hard
    - ○ soft

2. gym
    - ○ hard
    - ○ soft

3. gem
    - ○ hard
    - ○ soft

4. ginger
    - ○ hard
    - ○ soft

5. gutter
    - ○ hard
    - ○ soft

6. germ
    - ○ hard
    - ○ soft

7. goal
    - ○ hard
    - ○ soft

8. goat
    - ○ hard
    - ○ soft

9. gentle
    - ○ hard
    - ○ soft

10. giraffe
    - ○ hard
    - ○ soft

11. gerbil
    - ○ hard
    - ○ soft

12. gel
    - ○ hard
    - ○ soft

Hard and Soft G

Read each word. Color the boxes with hard *g* words green. Color the boxes with soft *g* words orange.

giraffe	gerbil	gem	germ	gate
gym	goat	gopher	guitar	gone
giant	good	gold	gown	goal
gel	gaze	genius	George	gill
general	gutter	game	gentle	gap
gypsy	genie	gentleman	ginger	gum

 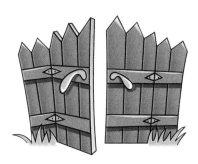 

Review: -LE Words and Hard and Soft C and G

To review words ending in -*le* and hard and soft *c* and *g* words, read the story. Write the word that completes each sentence on the line.

Johnny Appleseed

Johnny put on his backpack. Then, he went out of the gate in his backyard. He kept a large cup of apple seeds inside his pack. He gave the seeds to nice people. In return, they gave him oatmeal to eat. The planted seeds grew quickly. The next day, the little trees grew into giant trees. There was an apple on everyone's table.

_____

_ _ _ _ _ _ _ _ _

1. Johnny went out of the _____ in his backyard.

_____

_ _ _ _ _ _ _ _

2. People were _____ and gave him food to eat.

_____

_ _ _ _ _ _ _

3. The seeds _____ quickly.

_____

_ _ _ _ _ _ _ _ _

4. An apple was on everyone's _____ .

_____

Consonant Blends: R

A consonant blend is two or more different consonants. The sound of each consonant blends, but you can hear each one.

Examples: gr–grape, br–brake, tr–tree

Say the name of each picture. Circle the correct word.

1.

brake   broom   bread

2.

brake   bring   branch

3.

grade   grass   grape

4.

from   fruit   frost

5.

trail   trade   truck

6.

drum   drive   drip

7.

price   press   prince

8.

free   frost   frog

9.

trike   trim   tree

Consonant Blends: L

Say each bold word. Listen to the blend. Find the words in the Word Bank with the same blend. Write the words in the correct columns.

Word Bank

clock	glass	glue	flag
plant	class	blue	slow
blow	flat	plane	slick

1. **glad**
_____

- - - - - - - - - -
_____
_____
_____
- - - - - - - - - -
_____
_____

2. **flame**
_____

- - - - - - - - - -
_____
_____
_____
- - - - - - - - - -
_____
_____

3. **close**
_____

- - - - - - - - - -
_____
_____
_____
- - - - - - - - - -
_____
_____

4. **plate**
_____

- - - - - - - - - -
_____
_____
- - - - - - - - - -
_____

5. **black**
_____

- - - - - - - - - -
_____
_____
- - - - - - - - - -
_____

6. **slip**
_____

- - - - - - - - - -
_____
_____
- - - - - - - - - -
_____

Consonant Blends: S

Say the name of each picture. Draw a line from the picture to its beginning blend.

sc

st

sp

sn

sw

sm

sl

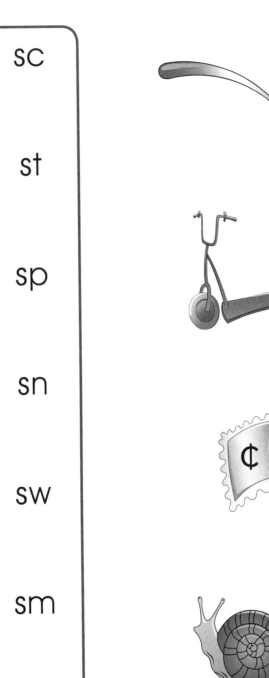

Final Consonant Blends

Say each set of words. Listen to the consonant blend at the end of each word. Circle the correct word to complete each sentence. Then, write it on the line.

1. We like to _____ in the woods.

   clamp
   camp

2. Our campsite has a large _____.

   stamp
   stump

3. It is my task to set up the _____.

   tent
   rent

4. We hang our water from the tree _____.

   bunk
   trunk

5. I need help taking the _____ to the river.

   raft
   left

Y as a Vowel

Sometimes, the consonant *y* sounds like the long vowel sound of *e* or *i*.

Examples: long *e*–puppy, long *i*–cry

Say the name of each picture. Circle the word below each picture that has the same *y* sound.

1.

dry   body   why

2.

daddy   spy   Ty

3.

happy   very   shy

4.

sandy   try   sleepy

5.

my   try   tiny

6.

sly   funny   by

Y as a Vowel

When *y* is at the end of a one-syllable word, it usually sounds like a long *i*.

Example: long *i*–sky

Say each word in the Word Bank. Underline the *y* words that have the long *i* sound. Then, circle each Word Bank word in the puzzle. Words can go across, up, down, or diagonally.

Word Bank

rocky	lucky	muddy	lily
hurry	cry	dry	fly
why	bunny	try	sky
spy	fry	shy	many

g	y	s	y	g	i	b	w	m	i
w	r	k	l	j	c	y	u	y	j
h	f	y	f	t	p	d	h	k	v
y	a	l	k	s	d	s	j	c	y
r	o	c	k	y	y	a	i	u	n
o	z	m	p	r	v	y	y	l	a
s	m	y	r	y	i	l	n	u	m
i	r	u	q	r	o	i	n	h	m
d	h	b	p	c	m	l	u	i	y
p	t	r	y	d	d	s	b	e	l

Review: Blends and Y as a Vowel

Use the words from the Word Bank to correctly finish the story. Write the word that completes each sentence on the line.

> **Word Bank**
>
> scream   trunk   sneaky   dress   try   stuck

1. "Let's play _____ up," said Blake.

2. Mandy got the dusty _____ from inside the closet.

3. " _____ to lift the lid with your hands," said Mandy.

4. "It's _____!" Blake said with an angry cry.

5. Suddenly, Ty jumped out with a _____ .

6. "That was a _____ trick," Mandy said with a smile.

Consonant Digraphs

A consonant digraph is two consonants together that make one sound. Say the name of each picture. Listen to the digraph. Find the words in the Word Bank with the same digraph. Write the words on the lines under the correct pictures.

Word Bank

thin	each	shake	shoe
white	wheel	this	beach

Consonant Digraphs

**Choose the correct word to complete each sentence. Circle the word.
Then, write it on the line.**

_____

— — — — — — — — — —

1. Sometimes, I like to _____ .

shop
sell
shape

_____

— — — — — — — — — —

2. This _____ is very nice to sit on.

chip
such
chair

_____

— — — — — — — — — —

3. I'm hungry. I wish it was time for _____ .

much
which
lunch

_____

— — — — — — — — — —

4. Sherry will _____ a nice shirt for Dad.

check
choose
bunch

_____

— — — — — — — — — —

5. She knows _____ I like to eat.

which
what
much

_____

— — — — — — — — — —

6. I reached for the fresh _____ .

chip
peach
change

_____

Consonant Digraphs

Say the words in each row. Listen for each word's digraph. Draw an X on the word in each row that does not have the same digraph.

1.	wash	sheep	shoe	this
2.	white	with	when	what
3.	thing	bath	peach	thick
4.	chick	cash	change	cheese
5.	south	with	thing	dish
6.	shut	shake	why	wish
7.	whistle	write	which	whale
8.	teeth	chimp	each	cherry

Silent Letters: K

The consonant digraph *kn* makes an *n* sound because the *k* is silent. Choose the *kn* word from the Word Bank that rhymes with each word. Write it on the line.

Word Bank					
knot	knock	knight	kneel	knee	know

1. feel

_____

2. blow

_____

3. clock

_____

4. pot

_____

5. might

_____

6. free

_____

Silent Letters: W

The consonant digraph *wr* makes an *r* sound because the *w* is silent. Choose the best word from the Word Bank to solve each riddle. Then, write it on the line.

Word Bank

wrist	wren	wreath	wrinkles	wrench	wrap

1. People sometimes hang me on a door. _____

2. When you open a gift, you rip me off of the outside. _____

3. People iron me out of clothing. _____

4. Many people think I am a helpful tool. _____

5. People put a watch on me. _____

6. I am a tiny bird that eats insects. _____

Review Crossword

Read each clue. Then, find the word in the Word Bank that answers the clue. Write the word in the puzzle.

Word Bank

knee   cheese   write   beach   shells   teeth

Across

3. One of these is in the middle of your leg.
5. A mouse loves to eat this.
6. You brush these twice each day.

Down

1. You do this with a pencil.
2. This has a lot of sand and shells.
4. You find these on the beach.

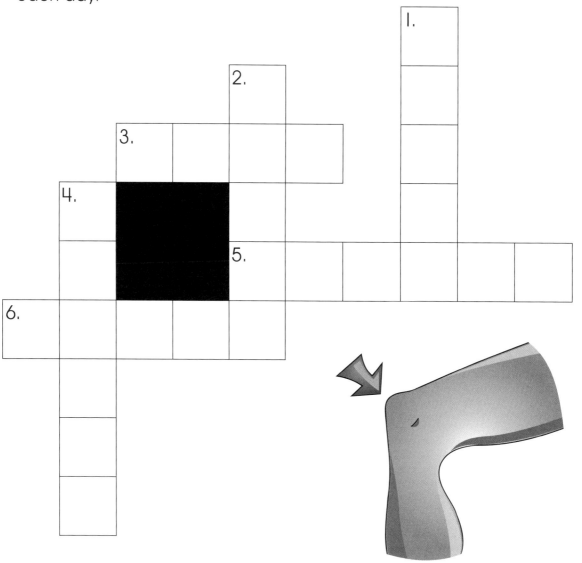

Words with -AR

When *r* follows the vowel *a*, it changes the sound that the vowel makes. The letter pair *ar* says the name of the letter *r*.

Examples: mark, tart

Say the word in each jar. Find the words in the Word Bank that rhyme with the word. Write the words on the lines under the correct jar.

Word Bank				
smart	lark	dark	card	park
part	yard	dart	lard	

hard

cart

shark

Words with -OR

When _r_ follows the vowel _o_, it changes the sound that the vowel makes.

Examples: for, nor

Say the four words in each box. Circle the word that does not rhyme. Then, write it on the line below the box.

```
┌─────────────────────────────┐
│   porch          born       │
│                             │
│   torch          scorch     │
└─────────────────────────────┘
```

1. _____

```
┌─────────────────────────────┐
│   horn           popcorn    │
│                             │
│   horse          torn       │
└─────────────────────────────┘
```

2. _____

```
┌─────────────────────────────┐
│   fort           porch      │
│                             │
│   short          sport      │
└─────────────────────────────┘
```

3. _____

```
┌─────────────────────────────┐
│   born           storm      │
│                             │
│   thorn          corn       │
└─────────────────────────────┘
```

4. _____

Write a sentence using some of the words you wrote.

_____

_____

_____

44

Words with -ER, -IR, and -UR

When *r* follows a vowel, it changes the sound the vowel makes. The letter pairs *er*, *ir*, and *ur* make the same sound.

Examples: her, first, purse

Read each word. Look for the vowel followed by an *r*. Then, draw a line from the word to the matching vowel + *r*.

her   skirt

burn   purr

                                    (er)

stir   after

third   turn

first   birth

turtle   (ir)   letter

shirt   fur

germ   nerve

curve   girl

                                    (ur)

chirp   curl

Review Words

Read this silly story. Then, read each word in the box and find the bold word in the story that rhymes with it. Write the number of the rhyming word in the blank.

I was sitting on the (1) **torch** the other night. It was very, very (2) **park** and

(3) **dormy**. Suddenly, a (4) **fork** came flying into the (5) **card**. "Help!" it said. "A

(6) **curl** is after me."

"Go to the (7) **more**," I said. "There is a (8) **force** waiting to take you

(9) **bar** away. Don't (10) **furry**, it will not (11) **dirt** you." Afterward, I (12) **burned** that

(13) **forks** are not very (14) **dart**!

_____ horse	_____ smart	_____ storks	_____ shore	_____ girl
_____ porch	_____ hurt	_____ far	_____ yard	_____ stork
_____ dark	_____ stormy	_____ worry	_____ learned	

Contractions: will

A contraction is a way to make two words into one. To make the new word, one or more letters are left out. An apostrophe (') is used to show where the letter or letters were taken out. Some contractions are made with the word *will*.

Do contraction subtraction: I + will – wi = I'll

Read each set of words. Then, choose a word from the Word Bank that can take the place of the two words. Write it on the line.

Word Bank					
I'll	they'll	you'll	she'll	we'll	he'll

1. you will

_____

— — — — — — — —

_____

_____

2. we will

_____

— — — — — — — —

_____

_____

3. he will

_____

— — — — — — — —

_____

_____

4. they will

_____

— — — — — — — —

_____

_____

5. I will

_____

— — — — — — — —

_____

_____

6. she will

_____

— — — — — — — —

_____

_____

Contractions: not

Some contractions are made with the word *not*.

Do contraction subtraction: is + not – o = isn't

Read each sentence. Then, underline two words in the sentence that could make one of the contractions in the Word Bank. Write the contraction on the line.

Word Bank				
isn't	don't	haven't	hasn't	didn't

1. Justin is sick and has not come to the park. _____

2. He did not get chicken pox when I did. _____

3. Now, Justin has red dots, and I do not. _____

4. Rosa and Wendy have not visited. _____

5. But, that is not going to stop me. _____

48

Contractions: is

Some contractions are made with the word *is*.

Do contraction subtraction: it + is – i = it's

Read each sentence. Look at each bold contraction. Then, write the two words that make the contraction on the lines with the same number.

1. "**Where's** your tarantula?" I asked Whitney.
2. "I think **she's** lost somewhere under my bed."
3. "**That's** too bad," I said as I turned to run.
4. "Hey, **what's** your hurry, Marci? It was just a joke. She's in her tank."

1. _____ + _____

2. _____ + _____

3. _____ + _____

4. _____ + _____

Contractions: have

**Read each sentence. Do contraction subtraction with the words in bold.
Then, write the contraction on the line.**

1. Corinne, **I have** taken a picture of the mom and her baby.

   — — — — — — + — — — — — — – ha = — — — — — —

2. **You have** worked hard today.

   — — — — — — + — — — — — — – ha = — — — — — —

3. **We have** seen plenty of deer before.

   — — — — — — + — — — — — — – ha = — — — — — —

4. **They have** returned to the forest.

   — — — — — — + — — — — — — – ha = — — — — — —

Contractions: am, are, and us

Some contractions are made with the words *am*, *are*, or *us*.

Do contraction subtraction: I + am – a = I'm
we + are – a = we're
let + us – u = let's

Read each sentence. Underline the contraction. Then, write the number of the sentence next to the two words in the Word Bank that make the contraction.

Word Bank

_____ Let us   _____ You are   _____ I am

_____ They are   _____ We are

1. "Let's go swimming in the lake," Patricia yelled.

2. "We're going to take Abbey too," Porter added.

3. "You're sure they let dogs on the beach?" Mom asked.

4. "I'm sure," said Emerson as they all ran to swim.

5. "They're always running around and barking."

Vowel Digraphs: -AI and -AY

When two vowels are together, the first vowel often makes the long vowel sound, and the second vowel is silent. The vowel pairs *ai* and *ay* make the long *a* sound.

Examples: pail, day

Circle the correct word to complete each sentence.

1. I like to see the (nail, snail, pain) move slowly on the wet grass.

2. It leaves a slimy (mail, wait, trail).

3. The brown shell on its back is very (pay, may, plain).

4. It may take all (clay, tray, day) for it to cross the yard.

5. But, I cannot (stay, pay, way) here and play.

6. Dad and I are going to (sail, paint, ray) the house.

7. We have a gray (pail, maid, stain) full of red paint.

8. I hope we finish before it starts to (chain, say, rain).

Vowel Digraphs: -EE and -EA

The vowel pairs _ee_ and _ea_ can make the long _e_ sound. Circle the correct word to complete each sentence. Then, write it on the line.

1. Yesterday, we went to swim in the _____.

    tree
    peep
    sea

2. It was cold, but the _____ loved it.

    jeans
    beans
    seals

3. Seals don't have _____. They have flippers.

    feet
    deep
    each

4. For their morning _____, they eat fish.

    seed
    meal
    jeep

5. I think it would be _____ to be a seal.

    easy
    seen
    three

6. They just bask in the sun on the _____.

    peach
    peal
    beach

Vowel Digraphs: -OE and -OA

The vowel pairs *oe* and *oa* can make the long *o* sound. Choose the correct word from the Word Bank to solve each riddle. Then, write it on the line.

Word Bank				
toe	goat	coat	doe	soap

1. I can be found on a foot.
    Do you know what I am?

    _____

2. You use me to wash your hands.
    Do you know what I am?

    _____

3. You put me on in the winter.
    Do you know what I am?

    _____

4. I am a female deer.
    Do you know what I am?

    _____

5. I live on a farm.
    Do you know what I am?

    _____

Vowel Digraphs: -EA

The vowel pair *ea* can make the short *e* sound.

Example: sweat

Choose the correct word from the Word Bank to complete each sentence. Then, write one letter of the word on each line.

Word Bank

bread	feather	heavy	breath
spread	ready	weather	head

---

1. To make toast, we use wheat ___ ___ ___ [ ] ___ .

2. I [ ] ___ ___ ___ ___ ___ grape jelly on with a knife.

3. In cold [ ] ___ ___ ___ ___ ___ ___ , we have hot chocolate.

4. Mom has it ___ [ ] ___ ___ ___ early in the morning.

5. Steve puts on his ___ ___ [ ] ___ ___ coat to go outside.

6. Carrie has a coat that's light as a ___ ___ ___ [ ] ___ ___ ___ .

7. Alex has a hat on his ___ [ ] ___ ___ .

8. I can see my ___ [ ] ___ ___ ___ ___ on the car window.

Write the letters from the boxes in order to answer the question, What can you wear when it is cold?

___ ___ ___ ___ ___ ___ ___ ___

Variant Vowels: -oo

The vowel pair *oo* can make two different sounds. The long *oo* sound is heard in *moon*. The short *oo* sound is heard in *book*. Say each word in the Word Bank. Write the word under the picture whose name makes the same sound.

Word Bank

cook	good	foot	food	hook
room	boot	spoon	wood	noon

© Rainbow Bridge Publishing

Diphthongs: -AU and -AW

The letter pairs *au* and *aw* make the same sound. It is a tired sound—like when you *yawn*.

Examples: caught, lawn

Look at each picture and say the word. Circle the word that names each picture.

1.

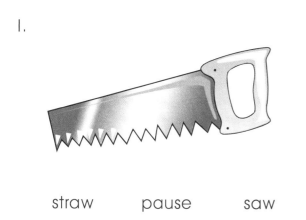

straw pause saw

2.

fault raw yawn

3.

haul auto paw

4.

autumn laundry crawl

5.

hawk because dawn

6.

applesauce claw fawn

Diphthongs: -OU and -OW

The letter pairs _ou_ and _ow_ can make the same sound.

Examples: cloud, crown

Read each sentence. Circle all of the words with _ou_ and _ow_ diphthongs. Then, write each word in the correct column below and on page 59.

1. We found our cat Scout just outside of town.

2. We are not sure how, but maybe it was his loud meow.

3. Now, he likes to hide behind the couch at our house.

4. Scout has a stuffed brown mouse.

ou

_____

- - - - - - - - - - - - - -

_____

_____

- - - - - - - - - - - - - -

_____

_____

- - - - - - - - - - - - - -

_____

ow

_____

- - - - - - - - - - - - - -

_____

_____

- - - - - - - - - - - - - -

_____

_____

- - - - - - - - - - - - - -

_____

Diphthongs: -OU and -OW

ou

_____

- - - - - - - - - - - -

_____

- - - - - - - - - - - -

_____

- - - - - - - - - - - -

_____

- - - - - - - - - - - -

_____

ow

_____

- - - - - - - - - - - -

_____

_____

Diphthongs: -OI and -OY

The letter pairs *oi* and *oy* make the same sound. Say the name of each picture. Then, write the correct word from the Word Bank on the line.

Word Bank

| boy | boil | oil | coins | toys | point |

1.

_____

2.

_____

3.

_____

4.

_____

5.

_____

6.

_____

Diphthongs: -EW

The letter pair _ew_ makes an _oo_ sound. Choose the correct word from the Word Bank to solve each riddle. Then, write it on the line.

Word Bank				
dew	stew	screw	new	chew

1. Who knew that this helps hold two boards together?

   _____

2. Who knew that this is a thick soup with carrots and beef?

   _____

3. Who knew that when you eat, you do this with your teeth?

   _____

4. Who knew that this is water on the grass in the morning?

   _____

5. Who knew that this is the opposite of old?

   _____

Review: Vowel Digraphs and Variant Vowels

Say the name of each picture. Circle the letter pair that makes the vowel sound in each name.

1.

ea

oo

aw

2.

oo

ea

au

3.

ea

oo

aw

4.

au

oo

au

5.

oo

aw

ea

6.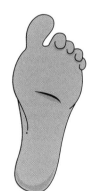

ea

oo

aw

Inflectional Endings: -ED

A base word is a word to which an ending can be added.

Example: rain + ed = rained

Read each sentence and the base word below the line. Add -*ed* to the base word. Then, write the new word on the line.

1. Larry _____ to see the parade.
   _____
   want

2. We _____ as the clowns passed by.
   _____
   laugh

3. They _____ in the air.
   _____
   jump

4. Then, the band played as they _____.
   _____
   march

5. We _____ when they waved.
   _____
   cheer

Inflectional Endings: -ING

A base word is a word to which an ending can be added.

Example: talk + ing = talking

Find the word with the *-ing* ending that matches each base word. Then, write the letter of the *-ing* word on the line.

1. _____ ask   a. kicking

2. _____ sleep   b. munching

3. _____ munch   c. pushing

4. _____ kick   d. sleeping

5. _____ push   e. asking

Add an *-ing* ending to each base word. Write the new word on the line.

6. find _____

7. want _____

8. play _____

9. snack _____

Review: Inflectional Endings

Find the word with the *-ing* or *-ed* ending that matches each base word. Then, write the letter of the *-ing* or *-ed* word on the line.

1. _____ roll   a. pushed

2. _____ dream   b. falling

3. _____ play   c. dreaming

4. _____ fall   d. rolling

5. _____ push   e. played

6. _____ bark   f. barked

Add an *-ing* or *-ed* ending to each base word. Write the new word on the line.

7. mark + ed _____

8. wish + ing _____

9. check + ed _____

10. break + ing _____

Two

Read the poem.

Two living things, blowing in the wind . . .
One barely moved, the other could bend.

One strongly rooted in the ground, growing tall.
The other, look closely, the blade is so small.

Both are so beautiful, Mother Nature's gift . . .
One you might climb, one you could lift.

Green is their color, brought on by spring.
Leaves or blades, they both make me sing!

Two

Use the poem (page 66) to answer each question.

1. What two things is this poem comparing?
    A. a tree and a swing
    B. a tree and a blade of grass
    C. a flower and a blade of grass

2. What color are both things?
    A. yellow
    B. blue
    C. green

3. Write the word from the poem that rhymes with each of these words.

    _____   _____

    — — — — — — — —   — — — — — — —

    tall _____   sing _____

    _____   _____
    _____

    — — — — — — —

    gift _____

    _____

4. Do you think that the poet likes the poem's topic? Why?

    _____

    —

    _____
    _____

    —

    _____

    _____

Firefly

Read the poem.

A little light is flying by,
is floating up to see the sky,
a little light with wings.

I never would have thought it,
to have a little bug all lit
and made to go on wings.

Firefly

Use the poem (page 68) to answer each question.

1. What is this poem about?
   A. the stars in the sky
   B. a firefly
   C. a bug with wings

2. Write the two pairs of rhyming words in this poem.

   _____   _____

   - - - - - - - - - -   - - - - - - - - - -

   _____   _____

   _____   _____
   _____   _____

   - - - - - - - - - -   - - - - - - - - - -

   _____   _____

   _____   _____

3. Who is the author of this poem?
   A. Jane Doe
   B. We do not know.
   C. Kim Carison

4. Have you ever seen a firefly? Draw one below.

Tulips

Read the poem.

In my flower garden, **tulips** always grow,
Straight like toy soldiers all in a row.

With colors so bright—reds, oranges, yellows, too,
They are one of nature's special gifts just for you.

Their colorful petals shaped like a cup
Hold little raindrops for birds to drink up.

Winds cause them to **sway**
Back and forth each day.

But still my tulips grow
Like toy soldiers in a row.

Tulips

Use the poem (page 70) to answer each question.

1. What is a tulip?
   A. a soldier
   B. a cup
   C. a flower
   D. a swing

2. How do tulips grow in this poem?
   A. slowly
   B. like toy soldiers in a row
   C. all over the place

3. Draw lines to match the rhyming words in this poem.

   grow   up
   day   row
   cup   too
   you   sway

4. What does *sway* mean?
   A. to move up and down
   B. to move side to side
   C. to stand still

5. Which word in the poem is a compound word?

   _____

   __ __ __ __ __ __ __ __ __ __ __ __ __

   _____

   _____

The Rain

Read the poem.

Pitter patter, pitter pat . . .
How I love the rain!

Storm clouds moving in,
The rain is about to begin.
How I love to see the rain!

Tiny sprinkles on my face,
Little droplets playing chase.
How I love to feel the rain!

I open up my mouth so wide,
Letting little drops inside.
How I love to taste the rain!

Tapping on my window,
It's a rhythm that I know.
How I love to hear the rain!

Everything looks so green,
And the fresh air smells so clean.
How I love to smell the rain!

Pitter patter, pitter pat . . .
How I love the rain!

The Rain

Use the poem (page 72) to answer each question.

Use the poem (page 72) to answer each question.

1. Draw a line to match each sense to the correct example from the poem.

   sight   fresh air

   touch   storm clouds moving in

   taste   letting little drops inside

   sound   tiny sprinkles on my face

   smell   tapping on my window

2. Circle the words that are adverbs. Underline the adjectives.

   slowly   quietly   fresh

   beautiful   gently   roughly

3. What goes "pitter patter"?
   A. rainbows
   B. raindrops
   C. clouds

4. Why does the air smell so clean in this poem?

   _____

   —

   _____

   _____

5. Do you like the rain? Why or why not?

   _____

   —

   _____

   _____

   —

   _____

   _____

The Snowman

Read the story.

It was a snowy day. Brandy and Alex decided to make a snowman. They bundled up and ran outside. First, they rolled a big snowball for the body. Then, they rolled a medium-sized snowball for the middle. Finally, they rolled a small snowball for the head. They stacked the three snowballs on top of each other. They found rocks for the eyes and mouth. They used a carrot for the nose. They used sticks for the arms. They were proud of their snowman.

74

The Snowman

Use the story (page 74) to answer each question.

1. What was the first thing Brandy and Alex did?
   A. They used a carrot for the nose.
   B. They rolled a big snowball for the body.
   C. They decided to make a snowman.
   D. They found rocks for the eyes and mouth.

2. What did Brandy and Alex use for the snowman's nose?
   A. a carrot
   B. sticks
   C. a rock

3. What is a compound word?
   A. two words put together to make a new word
   B. a word that describes an action
   C. a word that is used to name things

4. Circle all of the compound words in this story.

5. What would you name the snowman?
   _____

   —

   _____

   _____

My Dog, Eli

Read the story.

My dog, Eli, loves to go to the river. Every Saturday morning, I take Eli to the park by the river to play. The first thing Eli does when we get there is run to the water.

Eli likes to splash in the water. The cold water does not bother him. When he gets out of the water, he shakes and shakes. I stand back so that all of the water does not get on me. Then, he takes a nap on a rock. He sleeps there until I whistle for him when it is time to go home.

I think that our Saturday trips to the river are something that Eli looks forward to all week.

My Dog, Eli

Use the story (page 76) to answer each question.

1. What is the first thing Eli does when he gets to the river?
   A. He sleeps under a rock.
   B. He runs to the water.
   C. He splashes in the water.

2. Where does Eli take a nap?
   A. on my lap
   B. on the grass
   C. on a rock
   D. in the shade

3. Circle the words with short vowel sounds. Underline the words with long vowel sounds.

sun	splash
week	sleeps
rock	in
likes	Eli

4. How do you know when dogs are happy?

   _____

   _ _ _ _ _ _ _ _ _ _ _ _ _ _ _ _ _

   _____

   _____

   _ _ _ _ _ _ _ _ _ _ _ _ _ _ _ _ _

   _____

   _____

The Pumpkin Farm

Read the story.

Every October, Mrs. Lee's class takes a field trip to the pumpkin farm. The class walks around the barnyard and through the barn. They see some animals. Then, they go on a hayride. A big tractor pulls a large cart of hay. On the hayride, they ride through the apple orchard where farm employees are picking apples. Later, the apples will be made into applesauce. After the hayride, the students go to the pumpkin patch. There are hundreds of pumpkins. Each student picks out a pumpkin to take home. Mrs. Lee's class always has fun at the pumpkin farm.

78

The Pumpkin Farm

Use the story (page 78) to answer each question.

1. Why are farm employees picking apples on this farm?
    A. to make applesauce
    B. to sell at the market
    C. to make pies to eat

2. Underline the words with short vowel sounds. Circle the words with long vowel sounds.

Lee	trip	apples	patch
pumpkin	hay	ride	after

3. Use the bold words to make a compound word to complete each sentence.
    A **ride** in the **hay** is called a

    _____

    — — — — — — — — — — — — — — — — — —

    _____,

    A **sauce** made from an **apple** is called

    _____

    — — — — — — — — — — — — — — — — — —

    _____,

    The **yard** around a **barn** is called a

    _____

    — — — — — — — — — — — — — — — — — —

    _____,

4. What is your favorite thing to do with a pumpkin? Draw it on a separate sheet of paper.

Sing a Song of Summer

Read the poem.

Sing a song of summer,
Your arms stretched out wide.
You run in the sunshine.
You play all day outside.

Hold on to the summer
as long as you may.
Autumn will come quickly
and shorten the day.

So, play in the water,
roll in the grass.
It won't be long now
before you'll be in class.

Sing a Song of Summer

Use the poem (page 80) to answer each question.

1. What season is this poem about?
   A. summer
   B. spring
   C. autumn
   D. winter

2. What season will come quickly?
   A. summer
   B. spring
   C. autumn
   D. winter

3. There are eight words in this poem that have two syllables. Can you find them all? Write them on the lines.

The Koala

Read the passage.

Have you ever seen a koala? Most koalas live in Australia. They eat leaves from eucalyptus trees. They can eat more than three pounds (1.36 kg) of leaves in one day! Many people think that koalas are bears, but they are not. Koalas are marsupials. Marsupials are a special kind of mammal. Female marsupials have pouches on their stomachs to keep their babies warm and safe. If you cannot visit Australia, you might see a koala at your local zoo.

The Koala

Use the passage (page 82) to answer each question.

1. Where do most koalas live?
   A. in Africa
   B. in Australia
   C. in your neighborhood
   D. in Canada

2. What do koalas eat?
   A. eucalyptus leaves
   B. evergreen trees
   C. hamburgers
   D. walnuts

3. Write *T* in the blank if the sentence is true. Write *F* in the blank if the sentence is false.

   _____ Koalas eat fish.

   _____ Female marsupials have pouches to keep their babies safe.

   _____ Koalas eat only two leaves a day.

   _____ Koalas are bears.

4. What other animals can you think of that are marsupials? If you need to, ask a family member for help or check your local library.

   _____

   _____

   _____

   _____

   _____

   _____

Teddy

Read the poem.

Mom and Dad think I'm too old
to still have my teddy bear.
They say, "You are eight years old now,
and Teddy shows too much wear."
I nod my head and then agree.
I know I'm a really strong kid.
Without a thought, I put him up,
and in my closet he hid.

That same night, I tried and tried
but could not fall asleep.
A storm came in with so much noise,
but I did not make a peep.
Instead, I took my Teddy out
of the hiding place I'd made.
I did not need him to fall asleep.
I just knew he was afraid.

Teddy

Use the poem (page 84) to answer each question.

1. Why do Mom and Dad ask the poem's author to put away Teddy?
   A. They think Teddy is silly.
   B. They think the author will want to play with other toys instead.
   C. They think the author will lose the bear.
   D. They think the author is too old to have a teddy bear.

2. The author cannot fall asleep. Why?
   A. The storm is too loud.
   B. The author wants to stay awake.
   C. The author does not want to have bad dreams.

3. What happens when the author cannot sleep?
   A. The author gets out the teddy bear.
   B. The author calls for Mom and Dad.
   C. The author reads a story.

4. Who do you think was really afraid in this story? What made the person feel better?

   _____

   _____

   _____

   _____

   _____

   _____

   _____

   _____

   _____

The Swamp

Read the story.

In the jungle, there was a swamp.

Five wild pigs tromped by. "It is hot," they squealed. So, into the swamp they went.

Four monkeys came swinging by. "It is hot," they chattered. So, into the swamp they went.

Three frogs hopped by. "It is hot," they croaked. So, into the swamp they went.

Two snakes slithered by. "It is hot," they hissed. So, into the swamp they went.

One big alligator wriggled by. "It is not hot," he grinned, showing his great big teeth, "but I am hungry." So, into the swamp he went.

Suddenly, out from the swamp came two snakes, three frogs, four monkeys, and five wild pigs. It did not feel so hot anymore!

The Swamp

Use the story (page 86) to answer each question.

1. Why did the animals get out of the swamp?
    A. They did not want the alligator to eat them.
    B. It was too full.
    C. They were not hot anymore.

2. Draw a line to match each animal to the word that describes how it talked in this story.

    wild pigs   croaked

    monkeys   hissed

    frogs   chattered

    snakes   squealed

3. Write *T* in the blank if the sentence is true. Write *F* in the blank if the sentence is false.

    _____ The alligator was hot.

    _____ The alligator was hungry.

    _____ The frogs were hot.

    _____ The monkeys were hot.

    _____ The snake was hungry.

    _____ There were five wild pigs.

Insects

Read the passage.

Insects can be many different shapes and sizes. But, all insects have some things in common. Every insect has three main body parts. All insects have a head, a body that is called a **thorax**, and an abdomen. All insects have six legs. Most insects have two feelers on their heads called antennae. Many insects use their antennae to see, taste, and hear.

Insects

Use the passage (page 88) to answer each question.

1. How many legs does an insect have?
   A. six
   B. eight
   C. four

2. What is a *thorax*?
   A. an abdomen
   B. a body
   C. a leg
   D. an antennae

3. Write *T* in the blank if the sentence is true. Write *F* in the blank if the sentence is false.

   _____ All insects have nine legs.

   _____ All insects have an abdomen.

   _____ Insects come in different sizes.

4. What do insects use their antennae for?
   A. to listen to music
   B. to see, taste, and hear
   C. to create dances

Opposites

Read the poem.

My brother and I are opposites.
Believe me, because it is true.

I have green eyes, but
My brother's eyes are blue.

When I sit, my brother stands.
I sunburn easily, but he tans.

I am quiet. He is loud.
I am **humble**. He is proud.

I like soft music. He likes rock.
I like to sing. He likes to talk.

Although we are opposites to the end,
My brother is always my best friend.

Opposites

Use the poem (page 90) to answer each question.

1. What is the main idea?
   A. It is OK to be different.
   B. The author sunburns easily.
   C. The author's brother has blue eyes and tans well.

2. Write the opposite of each word on the line according to the poem.

   _____   _____

   — — — — — — —   — — — — — — —

   sing _____   sit _____

   _____   _____

   — — — — — —   — — — — — —

   loud _____   proud _____

   _____   _____

3. What is a synonym for *humble*?
   A. proud
   B. silly
   C. modest

4. In what ways are you and your best friend different? In what ways are you
   both the same?

   _____

   —

   _____

   _____

   —

   _____

   _____

The Library

Read the poem.

Behind my door, adventures are free,
so open it quietly and come to me.
I am a library, and through my door
are shelves and shelves of books **galore**.
Books can take you anywhere;
just open the cover and you'll be there.
They can take you into the sky or outer space,
or into the ocean, a deep, deep place.
They can take you into beaches with the whitest sands,
to long-ago times, or **distant lands**.
Read the opened books to see
how exciting the world can really be!

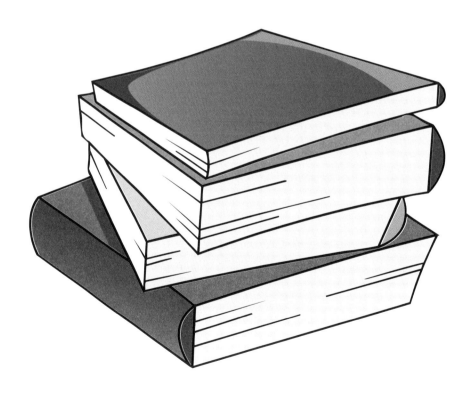

The Library

Use the poem (page 92) to answer each question.

1. What is the main idea of this poem?
   A. The library is a great place to go for adventure.
   B. The ocean is a deep place.
   C. The library has a lot of books.

2. What does *distant lands* mean?
   A. next door
   B. faraway places
   C. nowhere

3. What does *galore* mean?
   A. a lot
   B. a few
   C. some

4. How can books take you anywhere?

   _____

   _ _ _ _ _ _ _ _ _ _ _ _ _ _ _ _ _

   _____

   _____

   _ _ _ _ _ _ _ _ _ _ _ _ _ _ _ _ _

   _____

   _____

   _ _ _ _ _ _ _ _ _ _ _ _ _ _ _ _ _

   _____

   _____

Challenge: Compound Words

Can you find a match? To make a compound word, draw a line from each caterpillar to its chrysalis. Read the compound word in each butterfly. Then, draw a line from each word pair to the matching compound word butterfly.

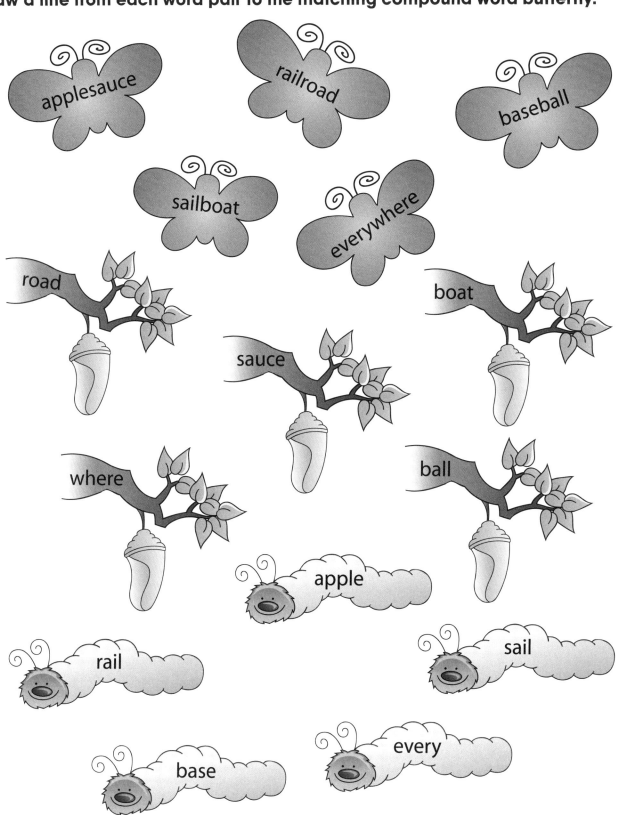

Challenge: Homophones

Homophones are words that sound the same, but are spelled differently and have different meanings. Read the six pairs of homophones in the Word Bank. Then, circle the homophones in the puzzle. Words can go across, up, down, or diagonally.

Word Bank

blew	weak	see
blue	week	sea
ate	son	pear
eight	sun	pair

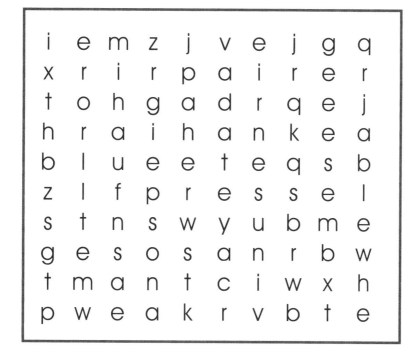

```
i  e  m  z  j  v  e  j  g  q
x  r  i  r  p  a  i  r  e  r
t  o  h  g  a  d  r  q  e  j
h  r  a  i  h  a  n  k  e  a
b  l  u  e  e  t  e  q  s  b
z  l  f  p  r  e  s  s  e  l
s  t  n  s  w  y  u  b  m  e
g  e  s  o  s  a  n  r  b  w
t  m  a  n  t  c  i  w  x  h
p  w  e  a  k  r  v  b  t  e
```

Challenge: Word Addition

Say the names of the pictures in each pair. Add the names together to write a new compound word on the line.

Think of a compound word. Draw a picture of each word and write the compound word on the line.

_____

\+　　　　　　　　　= _ _ _ _ _ _ _ _ _ _ _

_____

_____

Challenge: Treasure Hunt

Can you find the hidden treasure? Look at the map (pages 98–99). Read the clues and follow the instructions carefully to find where the treasure is buried.

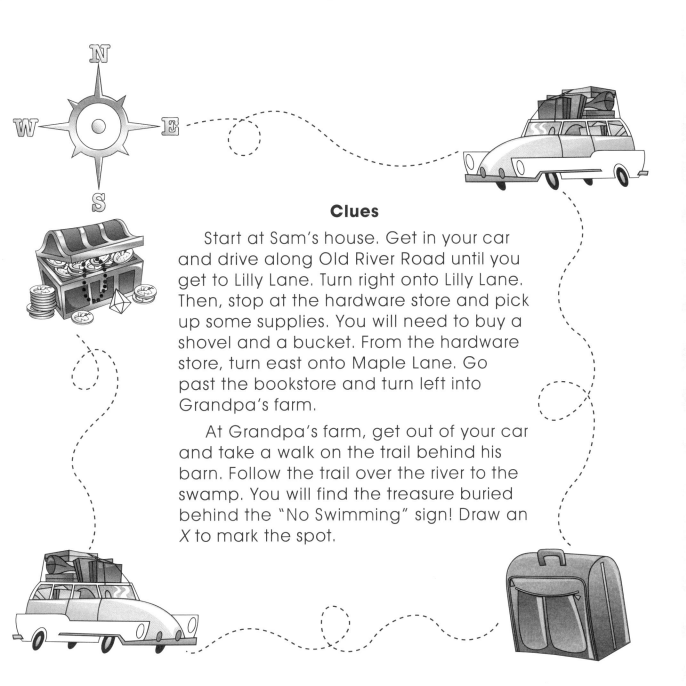

Clues

Start at Sam's house. Get in your car and drive along Old River Road until you get to Lilly Lane. Turn right onto Lilly Lane. Then, stop at the hardware store and pick up some supplies. You will need to buy a shovel and a bucket. From the hardware store, turn east onto Maple Lane. Go past the bookstore and turn left into Grandpa's farm.

At Grandpa's farm, get out of your car and take a walk on the trail behind his barn. Follow the trail over the river to the swamp. You will find the treasure buried behind the "No Swimming" sign! Draw an X to mark the spot.

Challenge: Treasure Hunt

Use the map to complete the exercises (pages 97–100).

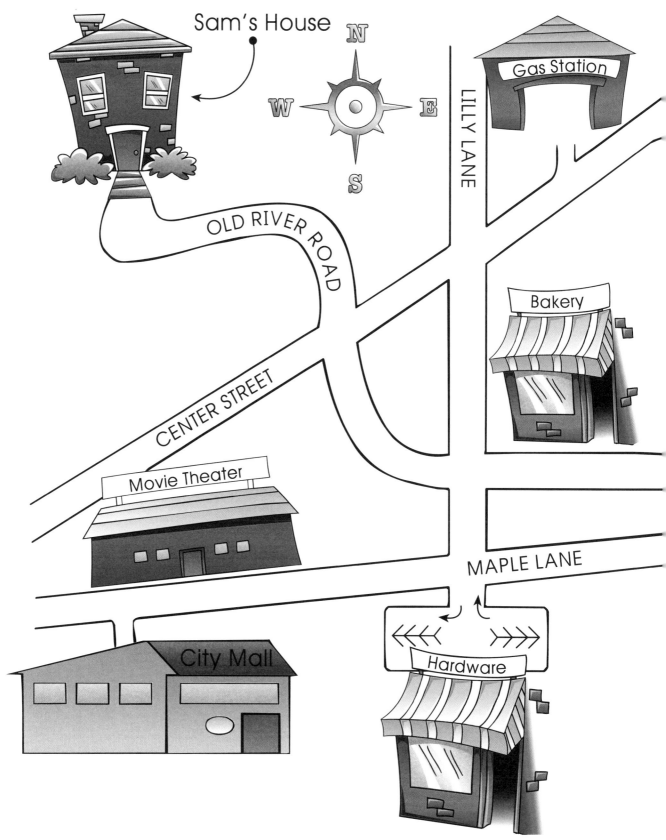

Sam's House

N
W   E
S

Gas Station

LILLY LANE

OLD RIVER ROAD

Bakery

CENTER STREET

Movie Theater

MAPLE LANE

City Mall

Hardware

Challenge: Treasure Hunt

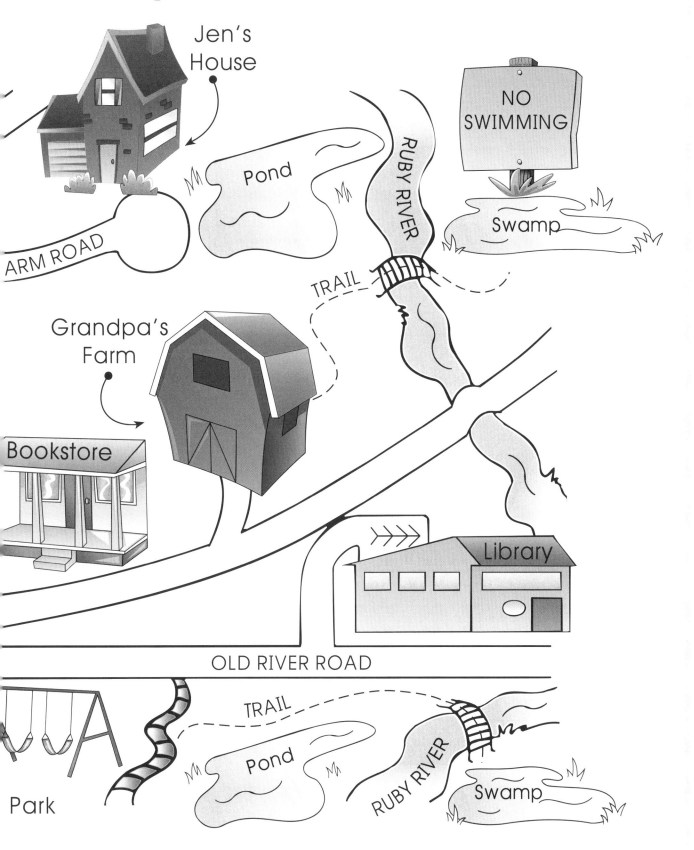

Challenge: Treasure Hunt

Use the map (pages 98–99) to answer each question.

1. What is the shortest way to drive from Jen's house to the library?

2. Did you pass Sam's house to get to the library?

3. Did you pass a park?

4. In which direction did you drive on Lilly Lane?
   A. north
   B. south
   C. east
   D. west

Challenge: Crossword

Read the clues. Then, complete the crossword puzzle.

Across

1. homophone for *eight*

4. A pot of gold is at the end of the _____.

7. synonym for *the same*

Down

1. Birds fly in the _____.

2. opposite of *nowhere*

3. We watched the _____ on Independence Day.

5. homophone for *blew*

6. We have fun together. We are best _____.

Challenge: Pet Show

Read the story.

Today is the neighborhood pet show. Holly, Amanda, John, and Greg have brought their pets. Use the clues to match each child to the correct pet.

Greg's pet likes to chase the girl's cat.

Holly's pet sings from its perch.

John's pet runs around on a wheel in its cage.

**Write an *X* in the box when you know that an animal does not belong to a child.
Write an *O* when you know that an animal does belong to a child.**

	Cat	Dog	Gerbil	Bird
Holly				
Amanda				
John				
Greg				

Challenge: Pet Show

Use the story (page 102) to answer each question.

1. Who brought their pets?

   _____   _____

   _ _ _ _ _ _ _ _ _ _   _ _ _ _ _ _ _ _ _ _

   _____   _____

   _____   _____

   _ _ _ _ _ _ _ _ _ _   _ _ _ _ _ _ _ _ _ _

   _____   _____

2. Draw a line to match each child to the correct pet.

   Holly   dog
   Greg   cat
   John   bird
   Amanda   gerbil

3. Which of these four animals would you like most for a pet? Why?

   _____

   _

   _____

   _____

   _

   _____

   _____

   _

   _____

Challenge: Present Mix-Up

Read the story.

Today is Rachel's birthday. She invited four friends to her party. Each friend brought a present. Rachel's little brother mixed up the tags on the presents. Use the clues to put the tags on the right presents.

Kelly's present has flowered wrapping paper and a bow.

Kate's present is square and has a bow.

Meg forgot the bow on her present.

Lisa's present has striped wrapping paper.

Write an *X* in the box when you know that a present does not belong to one of the girls. Write an *O* when you know that a present does belong to one of the girls. Then, draw the four gifts in the space provided.

	Square, striped with bow	Square, flowered with bow	Square, flowered without bow	Rectangle, striped with bow
Kate				
Kelly				
Lisa				
Meg				

Challenge: Present Mix-Up

Use the story (page 104) to answer each question.

1. Whose party is it?
   A. Rachel's
   B. Kelly's
   C. Meg's
   D. Lisa's

2. Whose present does not have a bow?
   A. Lisa's
   B. Meg's
   C. Rachel's
   D. Kate's

3. Who did not bring a present?
   A. Lisa
   B. Kate
   C. Kelly
   D. Rachel
   E. Meg

4. What do you think is inside each present? Draw a picture of each thing.

A Song for My Son

Read the song.

Here is a song for my son. It's a **melody** for him. It's about the day my poor son rode away. My son rode on his bike down the road in the sun. He rode and rode down the road. He rode for a week until his knees felt weak. Then, he pressed on his brake to take a break. He ate eight pairs of pears. Then, he blew a big blue bubble. That night as the sun set, my son became a knight.

A Song for My Son

Use the song (page 106) to answer each question.

1. What is a melody?
   A. a story
   B. a song
   C. a poem

2. What did the son eat?
   A. eight pairs of pears
   B. a pear of pairs
   C. eight pear of pairs
   D. a pair of pears

3. Circle the correct homophone in each sentence.

   The boys (ate, eight) everyone's dessert.

   The (sun, son) rises in the east.

   The sky is (blew, blue).

   I have a new (pair, pear) of pants.

4. Write a homophone for each word.

   break _____   ate _____

   sun _____   pair _____

   week _____   blew _____

The Gigantic Cookie

Read the story.

My mother baked a **gigantic** cookie for me. I sat on our porch to eat it. But, before I took a bite, my friend Anna came by.

"Will you share your cookie with me?" Anna asked. I broke my cookie into two pieces, one for me and one for Anna. But, before we took a bite, Jesse and Lucy came by.

"Will you share your cookie with us?" they asked. Anna and I each broke our cookie pieces into two pieces. Now, we had four pieces: one for me, one for Anna, one for Jesse, and one for Lucy. But, before we took a bite, four more friends came by.

"Will you share your cookie with us?" they asked. Anna, Jesse, Lucy, and I all broke our pieces in half. Now, we had enough to share between eight friends. But, before we took a bite, eight more friends came by.

"Will you share your cookie with us?" they asked. We all broke our pieces in half to share with our eight new friends. I looked at my gigantic cookie. It was no longer gigantic. "Hey, does anyone know what is gigantic when there's one but small when there are sixteen?" I asked.

"No, what?" my friends asked.

"My cookie," I laughed.

The Gigantic Cookie

Use the story (page 108) to answer each question.

1. What happens in the story?
    A.   Sixteen people share a cookie.
    B.   Mom buys a gigantic cookie.
    C.   The cookie is terrible.

2. Number each event in the order in which it happened.

    _____ Jesse and Lucy come by.

    _____ Mother bakes a cookie.

    _____ Four friends come by.

    _____ Anna comes by.

    _____ Eight friends come by.

3. What does *gigantic* mean?
    A.   small
    B.   huge
    C.   tiny
    D.   fat

4. With whom would you share a gigantic cookie?

    _____

    _

    _____
    _____

    _

    _____

    _____

The Gift

Read the story.

"Happy Mother's Day," Nathan said. He gave his mother a large box with a pretty bow.

"What is it?" his mother asked.

"You have to guess," Nathan said. "I'll give you a hint. It's soft and blue."

"Can I wear it?" asked his mother.

"Yes," said Nathan.

"I think I know," his mother said.

She opened the box. "Thank you, it is just what I asked for," she said.

Nathan's mother took the gift out of the box. She put it on over her head. She put her arms in the sleeves. It fit just right. Nathan's mother gave him a big hug.

110

The Gift

Use the story (page 110) to answer each question.

1. What did Nathan's mother receive?
   - A. a necklace
   - B. a sweater
   - C. a scarf

2. Why did Nathan give his mother a gift?
   - A. It was her birthday.
   - B. It was Mother's Day.
   - C. It was Christmas.

3. The words *he*, *she*, and *it* each take the place of a person or thing in the story. Write the answer to each question on the line.

   He gave his mother a large box. Who is *he*?

   _____

   _____

   _____

   She opened the box. Who is *she*?

   _____

   _____

   _____

   She put it on over her head. What is *it*?

   _____

   _____

   _____

4. On a separate sheet of paper, draw a picture of the present Nathan gave to his mother.

The Right Pet

Read the story.

"Please, Mom. May I please have a pet of my own?" asked Jackie.

"Well, you have shown that you can be **responsible**. I guess it is time you that had your own pet," said Mother.

"Hurray! Let's go!" shouted Jackie.

"But, first, you need to think about the right pet," said Mother.

"The right pet? I don't understand," said Jackie.

"The right pet is the right one for you. The right pet is the right size. You need to think about where you will keep your pet. You need to think about how much time you have to take care of it," explained Mother.

"Well," said Jackie. "We live in an apartment, so I guess my pet will need to be small. I want a pet that I can hold. I want a pet that I can **cuddle** with."

"Now, you're thinking," said Mother. "Let's go see what we can find."

Jackie and her mom went to the pet store. Jackie said to the pet store owner, "I am looking for a small, furry pet that I can hold." The pet store owner showed Jackie a puppy. The puppy was small and furry. But, Jackie knew it would not always be small. It would grow up to be a big dog. Jackie looked at a goldfish. "No good," she said. "I can't hold it." Finally, Jackie saw a gerbil. "This is perfect. It is small. I can hold it. It has fur. I can cuddle with it. This is the right pet for me," said Jackie.

Jackie took the pet home. Now, Jackie's only problem is deciding on just the right name for just the right pet.

The Right Pet

Use the story (page 112) to answer each question.

1. What does *responsible* mean in this story?
   A. to remember to feed and give water to the pet and clean its cage
   B. to remember only to feed the pet
   C. to feed the pet and clean its cage when you remember

2. Which of the following can be pets? Write an *X* on the line next to each pet.

   _____ elephant   _____ giraffe

   _____ parrot   _____ turtle

   _____ gerbil   _____ gorilla

   _____ rabbit   _____ kangaroo

   _____ cat   _____ mouse

3. Why does Jackie not want a goldfish?
   A. She does not like to swim.
   B. She wants a pet she can hold.
   C. The fish would not talk to her.

4. What does *cuddle* mean?
   A. to hold and hug
   B. to play with
   C. to jump with

My Pet Lamb

Read the story.

I have a pet lamb. She is little. Her mom cannot take care of her, so I do! I use a baby bottle to feed her warm milk. She sleeps in the barn on soft, clean hay.

I named my pet lamb Cotton because she is soft and white. I keep her clean by giving her baths with warm water and a soft rag. She does not like having her face and ears washed.

When the sun is shining, we go for walks in the field. Cotton likes to run around the field, smell the flowers, and watch the butterflies.

I try to play tag with her. Most of the time, she just wants to run after me. We have fun running together.

When we get tired of playing, we lie out in the sun and take short naps. I think she knows that I am her best friend. I know that I love her!

114

My Pet Lamb

Use the story (page 114) to answer each question.

1. What adjectives are used to describe Cotton?
   A. small and funny
   B. short and cute
   C. soft and white

2. What does Cotton not like?
   A. having her ears and face washed
   B. playing in the field
   C. sleeping in the sun

3. Write T in the blank if the sentence is true. Write *F* in the blank if the sentence is false.

   _____ Cotton is a lamb.

   _____ A lamb is a baby moose.

   _____ Cotton likes to eat dandelions.

   _____ Cotton likes to watch butterflies.

   _____ Cotton likes to sleep in the rain.

   _____ Cotton does not like to run.

4. Complete each word from the story by writing its ending on the line.

   _____   _____   _____

   _ _ _ _ _   _ _ _ _ _   _ _ _ _ _

   sleep _____   bott _____   wash _____

   _____   _____   _____

   _____   _____   _____

   _ _ _ _ _   _ _ _ _ _   _ _ _ _ _

   know_____   play _____   flower_____

   _____   _____   _____

Marvin the Moose

Read the story.

Marvin was a happy moose. He lived in the woods in Acadia National Park just outside Bar Harbor, Maine. Summer was Marvin's favorite time of year. From his favorite mountain, he could watch the tourists biking or watch the sailboats sailing into the harbor.

Marvin spent most of his time alone and was a little afraid of humans. However, his curiosity about the tourists in the town of Bar Harbor was just too much. Marvin **longed** to look into the shop windows and walk through the park of picnickers. He even dreamed about going on a whale-watching cruise!

Because it was unsafe to wander into town during the day, Marvin decided to try it at night. When he heard the town clock chime 10 times, Marvin began his journey into Bar Harbor. He peeked into the ice cream shop, where there was a young man mopping the floor. He wandered past the jewelry shop, admiring the sparkles and colors. Before he knew it, Marvin had walked onto the pier where many of the cruise ships docked.

Marvin admired the beauty of the Atlantic Ocean from the dock. He thought that he could see a whale in the distance. Just below, several crabs crawled along the sand.

Marvin was beginning to get tired. It was midnight. He decided that he was lucky that no one had spotted him and that he should go back home. Slowly, Marvin went back up the mountain and into the woods.

Marvin was very proud of himself for being so sneaky. "I walked all through town, and no one saw me!" Marvin thought. Marvin had sweet dreams as the people in the town below were getting ready for a new day.

Marvin the Moose

Use the story (page 116) to answer each question.

1. How does the story end?
   - A. Marvin is proud of his adventure.
   - B. Marvin gets on a boat and sails away.
   - C. The tourists ask Marvin to leave.

2. What is a synonym for *longed* in this story?
   - A. wished
   - B. cried
   - C. waited

3. Why was summer Marvin's favorite time of year?
   - A. He could watch the whales.
   - B. He could go biking.
   - C. He could watch the tourists and the sailboats.

4. Write a new ending for the story.

   _____

   _

   _____
   _____

   _

   _____

   _____
   _____

   _

   _____

   _____

How to Frost a Cake

Read the passage.

Jessica is making a cake for her mother's birthday. Her grandmother helped her bake the cake. But, her grandmother had to go home. She left these directions for Jessica.

1. Remove the cake from the baking pan and put it on a plate. To do this, place a plate face down on the cake. Then, flip over the cake and the plate. Remove the baking pan.

2. Open the frosting can. Spoon some frosting onto the middle of the cake.

3. Spread the frosting using the spreader. Always work from the center out to the sides. Add more frosting as needed. Spread the frosting evenly over the cake. Be careful not to press too hard, or you will tear the cake.

How to Frost a Cake

Use the passage (page 118) to answer each question.

1. What is the cake for?
   A. Grandmother's birthday
   B. a Christmas party
   C. Mother's birthday

2. What direction comes last?
   A. Spread the frosting evenly over the cake.
   B. Remove the cake from the baking pan.
   C. Spoon some frosting onto the middle of the cake.

3. What warning did Grandmother give Jessica?
   A. Do not lick your fingers.
   B. Do not use too much frosting.
   C. Do not share the cake with anyone.
   D. Be careful not to press too hard.

4. What is your favorite kind of cake? Write its name and draw a picture of it.
   _____

   _

   _____

   _____

Riding a Rainbow

Read the story.

Aaron would not go to sleep at night. Every night, he would ask his mom, "Can't I stay up just a little longer?"

One night, his mom asked him, "Why do you never want to sleep?"

Aaron answered, "Because I am afraid I will miss something!"

His mom laughed at that. "Don't you know that by staying up late, you are missing out on the most fun of all?" she asked.

"I am?" Aaron said.

"When you are sleeping, there is no limit to what you can do!" his mom said. "You can ride a rainbow on the back of a golden unicorn. You can talk to a leprechaun. You can travel through kingdoms and tell all of the dragons to brush their teeth! You can fly a plane or swim in the ocean. You can be best friends with monsters or meet a princess! You can do anything you want to in your sleep, and the best part is that you wake up right in your own bed every morning no matter what!"

Aaron thought about what his mom had told him. He thought about it all day long. Aaron was **skeptical** of his mom's idea. He was not sure it would work. That night, he thought that he would try it. Aaron went to bed on time. That night, he flew through space, played tic-tac-toe with aliens, and became a famous soccer player.

Now, he goes to bed early!

Riding a Rainbow

Use the story (page 120) to answer each question.

1. What is this story about?
   A. Aaron wants to be a famous soccer player.
   B. Going to sleep at night can be fun.
   C. Sleeping is bad for you.

2. How does Aaron get to do the fun things?
   A. by watching television
   B. by listening to his mom
   C. by dreaming about them

3. Aaron was skeptical of his mom's idea. What does *skeptical* mean?
   A. Aaron did not understand what his mom said.
   B. Aaron was not sure if his mom was right.
   C. Aaron thought it was a great idea.

4. What did you dream about last night? Draw a picture of your dream and write the story on a separate sheet of paper.

Who Is My Pen Pal?

Read the story.

For one year, I have been writing to a **pen pal**. A pen pal is a friend you write letters to. My pen pal's name is Max. He is in the second grade. He lives in Canada with his family. Today, Max is coming for a visit. I am going to meet him at the airport. I have never seen Max, so I'm not sure what he looks like. Max said to look for a boy with curly hair and glasses. Max said he would be wearing a baseball cap and carrying a backpack. Can you help me find Max?

122

Who Is My Pen Pal?

Use the story (page 122) to answer each question.

1. Circle Max (page 122).

2. Why does the author not know what Max looks like?
   A. He forgot.
   B. He has never seen Max.
   C. Max changed his hair color.

3. Write *T* in the blank if the sentence is true. Write *F* in the blank if the sentence is false.

   _____ Max has curly hair.

   _____ Max has glasses.

   _____ Max lives in the United States.

   _____ Max will not have a backpack.

4. What is a pen pal?
   A. a cousin that lives far away
   B. a person from Canada
   C. a friend you write letters to
   D. someone who gives you a pen

Changing Number Words to Numerals

Write the numeral for each number word.

A. one _____

    ten _____

    six _____

    four _____

    nine _____

B. thirty-one _____

    thirteen _____

    forty-three _____

    eighty-nine _____

    twenty-four _____

C. five _____

    zero _____

    eleven _____

    seven _____

    two _____

D. seventy-five _____

    twenty-nine _____

    sixty-seven _____

    eighteen _____

    sixty-eight _____

E. three _____

    fourteen _____

    thirty _____

    sixteen _____

    fifty _____

F. ninety-nine _____

    fifteen _____

    eighty-eight _____

    one hundred _____

    seventeen _____

Writing Numbers: 0-49

Write the numbers to 49. Start at 0.

0				4					
							17		
		22							
				35					
	41								

Use the chart to answer each question.

A. What number comes before 47? _____

B. What number comes before 11? _____

C. What number comes between 27 and 29? _____

D. What number comes after 32? _____

Writing Numbers: 50-99

Write the numbers to 99. Start at 50.

50					55				
	61								
				73					
								88	
				94					

Use the chart to answer each question.

A. What are the even numbers between 50 and 60?

   50, _____, _____, _____, _____, 60

B. What are the odd numbers between 81 and 91?

   81, _____, _____, _____, _____, 91

C. What is the next even number after 64? _____

Writing Numbers: 0-99

Write the numbers to 99. Start at 0.

0					5				
	11								
			23						
								38	
				44					
	62								
					85				
									99

Addition

Solve each problem. Write the sum.

A.
$$10 + 1$$ $$4 + 4$$ $$6 + 0$$ $$9 + 6$$ $$8 + 2$$

B.
$$5 + 4$$ $$11 + 0$$ $$2 + 1$$ $$5 + 2$$ $$10 + 4$$

C.
$$12 + 2$$ $$10 + 8$$ $$7 + 2$$ $$6 + 3$$ $$11 + 5$$

D.
$$6 + 2$$ $$11 + 2$$ $$1 + 0$$ $$4 + 5$$ $$12 + 7$$

E.
$$12 + 0$$ $$7 + 3$$ $$0 + 0$$ $$2 + 2$$ $$10 + 7$$

Subtraction

Solve each problem. Write the difference.

A. $\begin{array}{r} 9 \\ -\ 1 \\ \hline \end{array}$
$\qquad$ $\begin{array}{r} 10 \\ -\ 5 \\ \hline \end{array}$
$\qquad$ $\begin{array}{r} 7 \\ -\ 4 \\ \hline \end{array}$
$\qquad$ $\begin{array}{r} 6 \\ -\ 6 \\ \hline \end{array}$
$\qquad$ $\begin{array}{r} 8 \\ -\ 0 \\ \hline \end{array}$

B. $\begin{array}{r} 7 \\ -\ 7 \\ \hline \end{array}$
$\qquad$ $\begin{array}{r} 4 \\ -\ 3 \\ \hline \end{array}$
$\qquad$ $\begin{array}{r} 10 \\ -\ 3 \\ \hline \end{array}$
$\qquad$ $\begin{array}{r} 6 \\ -\ 4 \\ \hline \end{array}$
$\qquad$ $\begin{array}{r} 3 \\ -\ 3 \\ \hline \end{array}$

C. $\begin{array}{r} 9 \\ -\ 3 \\ \hline \end{array}$
$\qquad$ $\begin{array}{r} 10 \\ -\ 6 \\ \hline \end{array}$
$\qquad$ $\begin{array}{r} 12 \\ -\ 4 \\ \hline \end{array}$
$\qquad$ $\begin{array}{r} 5 \\ -\ 3 \\ \hline \end{array}$
$\qquad$ $\begin{array}{r} 6 \\ -\ 5 \\ \hline \end{array}$

D. $\begin{array}{r} 8 \\ -\ 2 \\ \hline \end{array}$
$\qquad$ $\begin{array}{r} 11 \\ -\ 7 \\ \hline \end{array}$
$\qquad$ $\begin{array}{r} 9 \\ -\ 4 \\ \hline \end{array}$
$\qquad$ $\begin{array}{r} 6 \\ -\ 3 \\ \hline \end{array}$
$\qquad$ $\begin{array}{r} 8 \\ -\ 5 \\ \hline \end{array}$

E. $\begin{array}{r} 7 \\ -\ 5 \\ \hline \end{array}$
$\qquad$ $\begin{array}{r} 8 \\ -\ 1 \\ \hline \end{array}$
$\qquad$ $\begin{array}{r} 9 \\ -\ 5 \\ \hline \end{array}$
$\qquad$ $\begin{array}{r} 12 \\ -\ 3 \\ \hline \end{array}$
$\qquad$ $\begin{array}{r} 11 \\ -\ 9 \\ \hline \end{array}$

Addition

Solve each problem. Write the sum.

A. $10 + 0 =$ _____

    $5 + 1 =$ _____

    $11 + 3 =$ _____

    $10 + 2 =$ _____

    $2 + 0 =$ _____

    $4 + 1 =$ _____

B. $8 + 6 =$ _____

    $12 + 1 =$ _____

    $1 + 1 =$ _____

    $9 + 5 =$ _____

    $10 + 3 =$ _____

    $9 + 2 =$ _____

C. $7 + 1 =$ _____

    $3 + 9 =$ _____

    $8 + 5 =$ _____

    $9 + 9 =$ _____

    $3 + 2 =$ _____

    $5 + 0 =$ _____

D. $6 + 0 =$ _____

    $11 + 8 =$ _____

    $8 + 8 =$ _____

    $12 + 2 =$ _____

    $10 + 10 =$ _____

    $7 + 5 =$ _____

Subtraction

Solve each problem. Write the difference.

A. $11 - 1 =$ _____

$9 - 7 =$ _____

$8 - 3 =$ _____

$10 - 3 =$ _____

$12 - 12 =$ _____

$9 - 0 =$ _____

B. $11 - 11 =$ _____

$10 - 9 =$ _____

$12 - 3 =$ _____

$4 - 0 =$ _____

$7 - 3 =$ _____

$8 - 1 =$ _____

C. $3 - 0 =$ _____

$11 - 4 =$ _____

$9 - 8 =$ _____

$12 - 1 =$ _____

$11 - 6 =$ _____

$6 - 3 =$ _____

D. $4 - 2 =$ _____

$12 - 5 =$ _____

$8 - 4 =$ _____

$5 - 5 =$ _____

$9 - 2 =$ _____

$11 - 10 =$ _____

Addition

Solve each problem. Write the sum.

A.
$$
\begin{array}{r} 7 \\ + 4 \\ \hline \end{array}
\qquad
\begin{array}{r} 7 \\ + 0 \\ \hline \end{array}
\qquad
\begin{array}{r} 10 \\ + 8 \\ \hline \end{array}
\qquad
\begin{array}{r} 4 \\ + 4 \\ \hline \end{array}
\qquad
\begin{array}{r} 3 \\ + 2 \\ \hline \end{array}
$$

B.
$$
\begin{array}{r} 11 \\ + 8 \\ \hline \end{array}
\qquad
\begin{array}{r} 8 \\ + 1 \\ \hline \end{array}
\qquad
\begin{array}{r} 9 \\ + 2 \\ \hline \end{array}
\qquad
\begin{array}{r} 6 \\ + 2 \\ \hline \end{array}
\qquad
\begin{array}{r} 4 \\ + 1 \\ \hline \end{array}
$$

C.
$$
\begin{array}{r} 9 \\ + 7 \\ \hline \end{array}
\qquad
\begin{array}{r} 0 \\ + 0 \\ \hline \end{array}
\qquad
\begin{array}{r} 5 \\ + 0 \\ \hline \end{array}
\qquad
\begin{array}{r} 8 \\ + 2 \\ \hline \end{array}
\qquad
\begin{array}{r} 9 \\ + 1 \\ \hline \end{array}
$$

D.
$$
\begin{array}{r} 5 \\ + 3 \\ \hline \end{array}
\qquad
\begin{array}{r} 1 \\ + 1 \\ \hline \end{array}
\qquad
\begin{array}{r} 7 \\ + 3 \\ \hline \end{array}
\qquad
\begin{array}{r} 6 \\ + 0 \\ \hline \end{array}
\qquad
\begin{array}{r} 12 \\ + 1 \\ \hline \end{array}
$$

E.
$$
\begin{array}{r} 10 \\ + 9 \\ \hline \end{array}
\qquad
\begin{array}{r} 5 \\ + 1 \\ \hline \end{array}
\qquad
\begin{array}{r} 10 \\ + 6 \\ \hline \end{array}
\qquad
\begin{array}{r} 7 \\ + 3 \\ \hline \end{array}
\qquad
\begin{array}{r} 10 \\ + 2 \\ \hline \end{array}
$$

Word Problems

Write a subtraction problem for each story. Then, solve each problem and write the difference.

A. Leanne fed the neighbor's dogs while they were on a trip. She fed 9 dogs in the morning and only 7 dogs at night. How many dogs did not eat at night?

B. Dianne planted 5 rosebushes in her flower garden. There were 3 red rosebushes. The rest of them were pink. How many rosebushes were pink?

C. There were 10 nuts on the ground. The chipmunks ate 7 of them. How many nuts were left on the ground?

D. Trent got a new box of 12 crayons. There were 6 broken crayons. How many crayons were not broken?

Addition and Subtraction: Mixed Practice

Solve each problem. Write the sum or difference.

A.
$$8 + 4$$ $$3 + 0$$ $$6 - 3$$ $$2 + 8$$ $$3 - 2$$

B.
$$10 - 5$$ $$2 + 2$$ $$6 + 2$$ $$9 - 8$$ $$5 - 4$$

C.
$$12 - 2$$ $$6 + 4$$ $$2 + 1$$ $$11 - 6$$ $$2 - 2$$

D.
$$7 - 4$$ $$7 + 0$$ $$10 - 8$$ $$4 - 4$$ $$3 + 2$$

E.
$$11 - 8$$ $$8 + 1$$ $$2 + 9$$ $$6 - 2$$ $$4 - 1$$

F.
$$4 - 2$$ $$11 - 7$$ $$9 - 4$$ $$12 - 9$$ $$1 + 5$$

Addition and Subtraction: Mixed Practice

Solve each problem. Write the sum or difference.

A. 4 + 3 = _____

   6 + 1 = _____

   12 − 11 = _____

   5 − 0 = _____

   4 + 7 = _____

B. 11 − 2 = _____

   2 + 9 = _____

   7 − 2 = _____

   8 + 2 = _____

   7 − 5 = _____

C. 5 + 5 = _____

   2 + 9 = _____

   9 − 0 = _____

   0 − 0 = _____

   8 − 4 = _____

D. 5 + 1 = _____

   6 − 4 = _____

   10 − 8 = _____

   9 + 3 = _____

   11 − 8 = _____

E. 10 − 0 = _____

   7 + 5 = _____

   9 − 6 = _____

   12 + 0 = _____

   9 − 5 = _____

F. 4 + 2 = _____

   6 − 2 = _____

   9 − 9 = _____

   4 + 7 = _____

   2 + 8 = _____

Word Problems

Write an addition or subtraction problem for each story. Then, solve each problem and write the sum or difference.

A. Mike rode his bike 6 miles on Monday and 5 miles on Tuesday. How far did he ride in all?

B. There were 8 bananas on a tree. A monkey ate 4 of them. How many bananas were left?

C. There were 9 children swimming. Three children went for a walk. How many children were there in all?

D. There were 12 boys on skateboards. Two of the boys fell down. How many boys did not fall?

E. Garrett had 11 model cars. He sold 8 to his friend. How many cars does Garrett have left?

Addition

Solve each problem. Write the sum.

A. 2 + 11 = _____

    8 + 7 = _____

    2 + 16 = _____

    0 + 14 = _____

    12 + 3 = _____

B. 16 + 1 = _____

    6 + 8 = _____

    9 + 8 = _____

    4 + 9 = _____

    7 + 6 = _____

C. 1 + 15 = _____

    7 + 10 = _____

    8 + 5 = _____

    8 + 8 = _____

    14 + 0 = _____

D. 17 + 1 = _____

    10 + 6 = _____

    6 + 12 = _____

    7 + 8 = _____

    12 + 5 = _____

E. 3 + 15 = _____

    15 + 1 = _____

    5 + 9 = _____

    3 + 10 = _____

    8 + 9 = _____

F. 18 + 0 = _____

    14 + 3 = _____

    9 + 7 = _____

    2 + 11 = _____

    6 + 9 = _____

Subtraction: Matching to Create Equations

Draw a line to match each problem with its difference.

A. 16 − 12 =   7   B. 18 − 2 =   13

    14 − 7 =   5   13 − 5 =   8

    18 − 17 =   4   15 − 2 =   9

    15 − 10 =   1   16 − 6 =   10

    13 − 11 =   2   18 − 9 =   16

C. 17 − 4 =   11   D. 16 − 16 =   12

    13 − 3 =   18   15 − 1 =   13

    16 − 5 =   10   17 − 5 =   14

    15 − 14 =   13   18 − 11 =   0

    18 − 0 =   1   13 − 0 =   7

E. 14 − 13 =   8   F. 18 − 13 =   12

    13 − 4 =   1   13 − 6 =   8

    16 − 9 =   9   16 − 4 =   4

    15 − 3 =   7   14 − 6 =   7

    17 − 9 =   12   15 − 11 =   5

Addition and Subtraction: Mixed Practice

Solve each problem. Write the sum or difference.

A.
$$\begin{array}{r} 1 \\ + 8 \\ \hline \end{array}$$
$$\begin{array}{r} 16 \\ - 6 \\ \hline \end{array}$$
$$\begin{array}{r} 15 \\ - 0 \\ \hline \end{array}$$
$$\begin{array}{r} 11 \\ + 4 \\ \hline \end{array}$$
$$\begin{array}{r} 15 \\ + 1 \\ \hline \end{array}$$

B.
$$\begin{array}{r} 5 \\ + 8 \\ \hline \end{array}$$
$$\begin{array}{r} 11 \\ + 3 \\ \hline \end{array}$$
$$\begin{array}{r} 18 \\ - 9 \\ \hline \end{array}$$
$$\begin{array}{r} 9 \\ + 5 \\ \hline \end{array}$$
$$\begin{array}{r} 16 \\ - 7 \\ \hline \end{array}$$

C.
$$\begin{array}{r} 17 \\ - 11 \\ \hline \end{array}$$
$$\begin{array}{r} 18 \\ - 0 \\ \hline \end{array}$$
$$\begin{array}{r} 11 \\ + 4 \\ \hline \end{array}$$
$$\begin{array}{r} 7 \\ + 6 \\ \hline \end{array}$$
$$\begin{array}{r} 16 \\ - 11 \\ \hline \end{array}$$

D.
$$\begin{array}{r} 18 \\ - 4 \\ \hline \end{array}$$
$$\begin{array}{r} 11 \\ - 3 \\ \hline \end{array}$$
$$\begin{array}{r} 8 \\ + 8 \\ \hline \end{array}$$
$$\begin{array}{r} 16 \\ - 9 \\ \hline \end{array}$$
$$\begin{array}{r} 14 \\ - 5 \\ \hline \end{array}$$

E.
$$\begin{array}{r} 14 \\ + 4 \\ \hline \end{array}$$
$$\begin{array}{r} 15 \\ - 12 \\ \hline \end{array}$$
$$\begin{array}{r} 8 \\ + 9 \\ \hline \end{array}$$
$$\begin{array}{r} 18 \\ - 12 \\ \hline \end{array}$$
$$\begin{array}{r} 6 \\ + 9 \\ \hline \end{array}$$

F.
$$\begin{array}{r} 10 \\ + 3 \\ \hline \end{array}$$
$$\begin{array}{r} 11 \\ - 7 \\ \hline \end{array}$$
$$\begin{array}{r} 14 \\ - 9 \\ \hline \end{array}$$
$$\begin{array}{r} 13 \\ + 5 \\ \hline \end{array}$$
$$\begin{array}{r} 15 \\ - 9 \\ \hline \end{array}$$

Writing Numbers: 100-149

Write the numbers to 149. Start at 100.

100									
		112							
					125				
							137		
				144					

Writing Numbers: 150-199

Write the numbers to 199. Start at 150.

150									
					165				
			173						
	181								
							197		

Writing Numbers: 100-199

Write the numbers to 199. Start at 100.

100									
							117		
				124					
			133						
					155				
									179
	181								
									199

Addition

Solve each problem. Write the sum.

A.
$$\begin{array}{r} 12 \\ +\ 7 \\ \hline \end{array}$$
$$\begin{array}{r} 13 \\ +\ 2 \\ \hline \end{array}$$
$$\begin{array}{r} 11 \\ +\ 16 \\ \hline \end{array}$$
$$\begin{array}{r} 14 \\ +\ 5 \\ \hline \end{array}$$
$$\begin{array}{r} 15 \\ +\ 12 \\ \hline \end{array}$$

B.
$$\begin{array}{r} 18 \\ +\ 1 \\ \hline \end{array}$$
$$\begin{array}{r} 14 \\ +\ 2 \\ \hline \end{array}$$
$$\begin{array}{r} 16 \\ +\ 3 \\ \hline \end{array}$$
$$\begin{array}{r} 11 \\ +\ 6 \\ \hline \end{array}$$
$$\begin{array}{r} 14 \\ +\ 10 \\ \hline \end{array}$$

C.
$$\begin{array}{r} 15 \\ +\ 13 \\ \hline \end{array}$$
$$\begin{array}{r} 13 \\ +\ 6 \\ \hline \end{array}$$
$$\begin{array}{r} 12 \\ +\ 2 \\ \hline \end{array}$$
$$\begin{array}{r} 15 \\ +\ 3 \\ \hline \end{array}$$
$$\begin{array}{r} 18 \\ +\ 10 \\ \hline \end{array}$$

D.
$$\begin{array}{r} 13 \\ +\ 10 \\ \hline \end{array}$$
$$\begin{array}{r} 14 \\ +\ 13 \\ \hline \end{array}$$
$$\begin{array}{r} 15 \\ +\ 4 \\ \hline \end{array}$$
$$\begin{array}{r} 14 \\ +\ 12 \\ \hline \end{array}$$
$$\begin{array}{r} 15 \\ +\ 2 \\ \hline \end{array}$$

E.
$$\begin{array}{r} 17 \\ +\ 11 \\ \hline \end{array}$$
$$\begin{array}{r} 15 \\ +\ 14 \\ \hline \end{array}$$
$$\begin{array}{r} 14 \\ +\ 1 \\ \hline \end{array}$$
$$\begin{array}{r} 17 \\ +\ 2 \\ \hline \end{array}$$
$$\begin{array}{r} 12 \\ +\ 4 \\ \hline \end{array}$$

Subtraction

Solve each problem. Write the difference.

A.
$$\begin{array}{r} 15 \\ -\ 8 \\ \hline \end{array}$$
$$\begin{array}{r} 13 \\ -\ 7 \\ \hline \end{array}$$
$$\begin{array}{r} 16 \\ -\ 4 \\ \hline \end{array}$$
$$\begin{array}{r} 18 \\ -\ 18 \\ \hline \end{array}$$
$$\begin{array}{r} 17 \\ -\ 6 \\ \hline \end{array}$$

B.
$$\begin{array}{r} 14 \\ -\ 11 \\ \hline \end{array}$$
$$\begin{array}{r} 16 \\ -\ 2 \\ \hline \end{array}$$
$$\begin{array}{r} 15 \\ -\ 15 \\ \hline \end{array}$$
$$\begin{array}{r} 13 \\ -\ 9 \\ \hline \end{array}$$
$$\begin{array}{r} 18 \\ -\ 5 \\ \hline \end{array}$$

C.
$$\begin{array}{r} 17 \\ -\ 0 \\ \hline \end{array}$$
$$\begin{array}{r} 16 \\ -\ 10 \\ \hline \end{array}$$
$$\begin{array}{r} 14 \\ -\ 3 \\ \hline \end{array}$$
$$\begin{array}{r} 17 \\ -\ 10 \\ \hline \end{array}$$
$$\begin{array}{r} 16 \\ -\ 0 \\ \hline \end{array}$$

D.
$$\begin{array}{r} 14 \\ -\ 7 \\ \hline \end{array}$$
$$\begin{array}{r} 15 \\ -\ 6 \\ \hline \end{array}$$
$$\begin{array}{r} 15 \\ -\ 11 \\ \hline \end{array}$$
$$\begin{array}{r} 12 \\ -\ 10 \\ \hline \end{array}$$
$$\begin{array}{r} 18 \\ -\ 2 \\ \hline \end{array}$$

Addition: Matching to Create Equations

Draw a line to match each problem with its sum.

A. 8 + 2 =   12   B. 8 + 10 =   9

    3 + 5 =   8   3 + 1 =   4

    5 + 2 =   17   7 + 7 =   14

    5 + 7 =   10   5 + 11 =   16

    8 + 9 =   7   6 + 3 =   18

C. 1 + 3 =   9   D. 7 + 2 =   13

    6 + 4 =   10   3 + 5 =   5

    1 + 8 =   4   8 + 6 =   9

    1 + 14 =   16   6 + 7 =   8

    3 + 13 =   15   1 + 4 =   14

E. 6 + 6 =   12   F. 2 + 3 =   12

    5 + 1 =   13   2 + 6 =   8

    7 + 6 =   6   3 + 4 =   4

    7 + 0 =   0   2 + 2 =   7

    0 + 0 =   7   10 + 2 =   5

Subtraction: Matching to Create Equations

Draw a line to match each problem with its difference.

A. 6 − 2 =   5   B. 14 − 13 =   8

    11 − 6 =   3   13 − 4 =   1

    8 − 7 =   4   16 − 9 =   9

    5 − 2 =   1   15 − 3 =   7

    3 − 1 =   2   17 − 9 =   12

C. 18 − 3 =   15   D. 16 − 1 =   1

    15 − 7 =   1   13 − 8 =   5

    14 − 4 =   8   16 − 15 =   12

    13 − 12 =   10   18 − 6 =   15

    16 − 8 =   8   17 − 7 =   10

E. 17 − 4 =   11   F. 16 − 11 =   1

    13 − 3 =   18   14 − 13 =   5

    16 − 5 =   10   18 − 8 =   9

    15 − 14 =   13   17 − 8 =   10

    18 − 0 =   1   14 − 1 =   13

Addition

Solve each problem. Write the sum.

A.
$$
\begin{array}{r} 15 \\ +\ 2 \\ \hline \end{array}
\qquad
\begin{array}{r} 16 \\ +\ 3 \\ \hline \end{array}
\qquad
\begin{array}{r} 14 \\ +11 \\ \hline \end{array}
\qquad
\begin{array}{r} 13 \\ +\ 4 \\ \hline \end{array}
\qquad
\begin{array}{r} 10 \\ +\ 7 \\ \hline \end{array}
$$

B.
$$
\begin{array}{r} 12 \\ +\ 4 \\ \hline \end{array}
\qquad
\begin{array}{r} 12 \\ +17 \\ \hline \end{array}
\qquad
\begin{array}{r} 13 \\ +\ 6 \\ \hline \end{array}
\qquad
\begin{array}{r} 12 \\ +\ 7 \\ \hline \end{array}
\qquad
\begin{array}{r} 13 \\ +\ 2 \\ \hline \end{array}
$$

C.
$$
\begin{array}{r} 18 \\ +11 \\ \hline \end{array}
\qquad
\begin{array}{r} 13 \\ +10 \\ \hline \end{array}
\qquad
\begin{array}{r} 14 \\ +\ 3 \\ \hline \end{array}
\qquad
\begin{array}{r} 18 \\ +\ 0 \\ \hline \end{array}
\qquad
\begin{array}{r} 17 \\ +\ 2 \\ \hline \end{array}
$$

D.
$$
\begin{array}{r} 18 \\ +\ 1 \\ \hline \end{array}
\qquad
\begin{array}{r} 14 \\ +14 \\ \hline \end{array}
\qquad
\begin{array}{r} 13 \\ +\ 3 \\ \hline \end{array}
\qquad
\begin{array}{r} 13 \\ +\ 1 \\ \hline \end{array}
\qquad
\begin{array}{r} 14 \\ +\ 3 \\ \hline \end{array}
$$

E.
$$
\begin{array}{r} 14 \\ +\ 2 \\ \hline \end{array}
\qquad
\begin{array}{r} 15 \\ +\ 4 \\ \hline \end{array}
\qquad
\begin{array}{r} 15 \\ +\ 1 \\ \hline \end{array}
\qquad
\begin{array}{r} 14 \\ +\ 3 \\ \hline \end{array}
\qquad
\begin{array}{r} 12 \\ +\ 5 \\ \hline \end{array}
$$

Subtraction

Solve each problem. Write the difference.

A.
$$17 - 11$$
$$18 - 0$$
$$11 - 4$$
$$7 - 6$$
$$16 - 11$$

B.
$$18 - 4$$
$$11 - 3$$
$$8 - 8$$
$$16 - 9$$
$$14 - 5$$

C.
$$14 - 4$$
$$15 - 12$$
$$9 - 7$$
$$18 - 12$$
$$9 - 6$$

D.
$$17 - 10$$
$$9 - 9$$
$$15 - 0$$
$$16 - 7$$
$$16 - 0$$

E.
$$18 - 6$$
$$15 - 10$$
$$15 - 5$$
$$16 - 6$$
$$12 - 3$$

F.
$$14 - 9$$
$$13 - 5$$
$$15 - 9$$
$$16 - 8$$
$$11 - 2$$

Word Problems

Solve each problem.

A. The students in room 9 go to school at 9:00. They go to lunch at 12:00. How many hours have they been in school before they go to lunch?

B. The students get out of school at 3:00. Joe had to leave at 1:00. How many hours of school did he miss?

C. Nineteen students each had to do a report. Eight students did reports on butterflies. How many students did not do reports on butterflies?

D. After recess, the students read silently. Scott read 12 pages, and his friend read 9 pages. How many more pages did Scott read?

Writing Numbers: 200-249

Write the numbers to 249. Start at 200.

200									
			213						
		222							
						236			
								248	

Writing Numbers: 250-299

Write the numbers to 299. Start at 250.

250									
								268	
				274					
						286			
290									

Writing Numbers: 200-299

Write the numbers to 299. Start at 200.

200									
				215					
	221								
			244						
						257			
		263							
								278	
		283							
									299

Reading Clocks

Look at each clock. Then, circle the correct time.

A. 3:00

    4:00

    12:00

B. 12:00

    4:00

    6:00

C. 7:00

    7:30

    8:30

D. 2:00

    12:00

    1:00

E. 6:00

    12:30

    2:00

F. 6:30

    10:30

    9:30

G. 11:00

    12:00

    10:00

H. 7:30

    8:30

    6:30

Clock Questions

Read each question and look at the clock. Write the answer on the line. The first problem has been done for you.

A. How many minutes are there from one number to the next? **5**

B. How many minutes are in one hour? _____

C. How many hours are on the clock? _____

D. How many minutes are in a half hour? _____

E. How many minutes are there from the 12 to the 3? _____

F. How many minutes are there from the 12 to the 7? _____

G. How many minutes are there from the 12 to the 9? _____

H. In one hour, the minute hand goes around the clock _____ time(s).

I. It takes the hour hand _____ hours to go around the clock.

J. How many hours are in one day? _____

Writing Time

Look at each clock. Then, write the time shown on the line.

A. _____

B. _____

C. _____

D. _____

E. _____

F. _____

G. _____

H. _____

Writing Time

Look at each clock. Then, write the time two ways. The first one has been done for you.

A. __10:10__ or __10__ minutes after __10__ o'clock

B. _____ or _____ minutes after _____ o'clock

C. _____ or _____ minutes after _____ o'clock

D. _____ or _____ minutes after _____ o'clock

E. _____ or _____ minutes after _____ o'clock

F. _____ or _____ minutes after _____ o'clock

Word Problems

Solve each problem.

A. The students in room 9 go to school at 8:00. They go to lunch at 11:00. How many hours have they been in school before they go to lunch?

B. The students get out of school at 3:20. Rick had to leave at 1:20. How many hours of school did he miss?

C. Liz began her homework at 4:00. She finished at 4:30. How many minutes did Liz work on her homework?

D. At 10:35, the teacher left the room. She was gone until 10:55. How long was she out of the room?

E. At 4:00, Lisa went to play with Dianne. Her mother said to come home in two and one-half hours. What time will Lisa go home? Show the time and write it on the line.

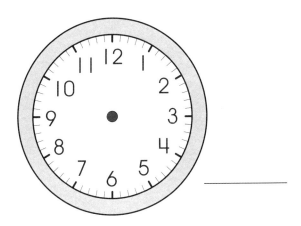

_____

Writing Numbers: 300-349

Write the numbers to 349. Start at 300.

300									
								318	
							326		
		332							
							347		

Writing Numbers: 350-399

Write the numbers to 399. Start at 350.

350						356			
	371								
				384					

Writing Numbers: 300-399

Write the numbers to 399. Start at 300.

300									
	321								
								348	
		353							
	392							399

Column Addition

Solve each problem. Write the sum.

A.
$$
\begin{array}{r} 6 \\ 2 \\ + 4 \\ \hline \end{array}
\qquad
\begin{array}{r} 5 \\ 1 \\ + 8 \\ \hline \end{array}
\qquad
\begin{array}{r} 2 \\ 2 \\ + 3 \\ \hline \end{array}
\qquad
\begin{array}{r} 9 \\ 3 \\ + 0 \\ \hline \end{array}
\qquad
\begin{array}{r} 8 \\ 8 \\ + 2 \\ \hline \end{array}
$$

B.
$$
\begin{array}{r} 7 \\ 2 \\ + 3 \\ \hline \end{array}
\qquad
\begin{array}{r} 3 \\ 6 \\ + 9 \\ \hline \end{array}
\qquad
\begin{array}{r} 0 \\ 4 \\ + 8 \\ \hline \end{array}
\qquad
\begin{array}{r} 10 \\ 3 \\ + 3 \\ \hline \end{array}
\qquad
\begin{array}{r} 6 \\ 4 \\ + 6 \\ \hline \end{array}
$$

C.
$$
\begin{array}{r} 6 \\ 4 \\ 2 \\ + 6 \\ \hline \end{array}
\qquad
\begin{array}{r} 1 \\ 1 \\ 9 \\ + 9 \\ \hline \end{array}
\qquad
\begin{array}{r} 2 \\ 7 \\ 2 \\ + 5 \\ \hline \end{array}
\qquad
\begin{array}{r} 1 \\ 8 \\ 3 \\ + 8 \\ \hline \end{array}
\qquad
\begin{array}{r} 0 \\ 0 \\ 9 \\ + 9 \\ \hline \end{array}
$$

D.
$$
\begin{array}{r} 6 \\ 5 \\ 2 \\ + 1 \\ \hline \end{array}
\qquad
\begin{array}{r} 9 \\ 0 \\ 5 \\ + 9 \\ \hline \end{array}
\qquad
\begin{array}{r} 6 \\ 7 \\ 2 \\ + 4 \\ \hline \end{array}
\qquad
\begin{array}{r} 7 \\ 1 \\ 3 \\ + 8 \\ \hline \end{array}
\qquad
\begin{array}{r} 3 \\ 9 \\ 2 \\ + 5 \\ \hline \end{array}
$$

2-Digit Addition without Regrouping

Solve each problem. Add the ones column first. Write the sum.

A.
$$24 + 11$$
$$16 + 12$$
$$32 + 21$$
$$16 + 23$$
$$19 + 20$$

B.
$$18 + 11$$
$$12 + 44$$
$$26 + 70$$
$$24 + 51$$
$$45 + 40$$

C.
$$17 + 52$$
$$23 + 43$$
$$73 + 24$$
$$12 + 14$$
$$25 + 14$$

D.
$$13 + 15$$
$$10 + 29$$
$$82 + 12$$
$$21 + 14$$
$$62 + 30$$

E.
$$25 + 10$$
$$22 + 22$$
$$11 + 24$$
$$14 + 24$$
$$36 + 11$$

F.
$$24 + 31$$
$$33 + 23$$
$$27 + 20$$
$$41 + 22$$
$$12 + 12$$

2-Digit Subtraction without Regrouping

Solve each problem. Subtract the ones column first. Write the difference.

A.
$$\begin{array}{r} 59 \\ -53 \\ \hline \end{array}$$
$$\begin{array}{r} 38 \\ -22 \\ \hline \end{array}$$
$$\begin{array}{r} 80 \\ -30 \\ \hline \end{array}$$
$$\begin{array}{r} 37 \\ -14 \\ \hline \end{array}$$
$$\begin{array}{r} 66 \\ -22 \\ \hline \end{array}$$

B.
$$\begin{array}{r} 27 \\ -24 \\ \hline \end{array}$$
$$\begin{array}{r} 72 \\ -21 \\ \hline \end{array}$$
$$\begin{array}{r} 33 \\ -20 \\ \hline \end{array}$$
$$\begin{array}{r} 60 \\ -20 \\ \hline \end{array}$$
$$\begin{array}{r} 39 \\ -17 \\ \hline \end{array}$$

C.
$$\begin{array}{r} 39 \\ -38 \\ \hline \end{array}$$
$$\begin{array}{r} 50 \\ -40 \\ \hline \end{array}$$
$$\begin{array}{r} 77 \\ -25 \\ \hline \end{array}$$
$$\begin{array}{r} 81 \\ -30 \\ \hline \end{array}$$
$$\begin{array}{r} 28 \\ -12 \\ \hline \end{array}$$

D.
$$\begin{array}{r} 94 \\ -82 \\ \hline \end{array}$$
$$\begin{array}{r} 63 \\ -43 \\ \hline \end{array}$$
$$\begin{array}{r} 36 \\ -34 \\ \hline \end{array}$$
$$\begin{array}{r} 25 \\ -20 \\ \hline \end{array}$$
$$\begin{array}{r} 47 \\ -16 \\ \hline \end{array}$$

E.
$$\begin{array}{r} 81 \\ -41 \\ \hline \end{array}$$
$$\begin{array}{r} 24 \\ -21 \\ \hline \end{array}$$
$$\begin{array}{r} 55 \\ -40 \\ \hline \end{array}$$
$$\begin{array}{r} 82 \\ -10 \\ \hline \end{array}$$
$$\begin{array}{r} 69 \\ -24 \\ \hline \end{array}$$

F.
$$\begin{array}{r} 99 \\ -35 \\ \hline \end{array}$$
$$\begin{array}{r} 75 \\ -45 \\ \hline \end{array}$$
$$\begin{array}{r} 42 \\ -31 \\ \hline \end{array}$$
$$\begin{array}{r} 96 \\ -33 \\ \hline \end{array}$$
$$\begin{array}{r} 73 \\ -52 \\ \hline \end{array}$$

2-Digit Mixed Practice without Regrouping

Solve each problem. Add or subtract the ones column first. Write the sum or difference.

A.
$$\begin{array}{r} 78 \\ -14 \\ \hline \end{array}$$
$$\begin{array}{r} 36 \\ +21 \\ \hline \end{array}$$
$$\begin{array}{r} 85 \\ +11 \\ \hline \end{array}$$
$$\begin{array}{r} 17 \\ +12 \\ \hline \end{array}$$
$$\begin{array}{r} 84 \\ -42 \\ \hline \end{array}$$

B.
$$\begin{array}{r} 20 \\ +20 \\ \hline \end{array}$$
$$\begin{array}{r} 75 \\ +22 \\ \hline \end{array}$$
$$\begin{array}{r} 60 \\ +30 \\ \hline \end{array}$$
$$\begin{array}{r} 95 \\ -41 \\ \hline \end{array}$$
$$\begin{array}{r} 84 \\ -62 \\ \hline \end{array}$$

C.
$$\begin{array}{r} 16 \\ +13 \\ \hline \end{array}$$
$$\begin{array}{r} 38 \\ -25 \\ \hline \end{array}$$
$$\begin{array}{r} 72 \\ +27 \\ \hline \end{array}$$
$$\begin{array}{r} 55 \\ -24 \\ \hline \end{array}$$
$$\begin{array}{r} 25 \\ +44 \\ \hline \end{array}$$

D.
$$\begin{array}{r} 75 \\ -54 \\ \hline \end{array}$$
$$\begin{array}{r} 10 \\ +10 \\ \hline \end{array}$$
$$\begin{array}{r} 20 \\ -10 \\ \hline \end{array}$$
$$\begin{array}{r} 18 \\ +21 \\ \hline \end{array}$$
$$\begin{array}{r} 62 \\ -51 \\ \hline \end{array}$$

E.
$$\begin{array}{r} 47 \\ -24 \\ \hline \end{array}$$
$$\begin{array}{r} 66 \\ -32 \\ \hline \end{array}$$
$$\begin{array}{r} 15 \\ +21 \\ \hline \end{array}$$
$$\begin{array}{r} 82 \\ +17 \\ \hline \end{array}$$
$$\begin{array}{r} 57 \\ -36 \\ \hline \end{array}$$

F.
$$\begin{array}{r} 62 \\ -60 \\ \hline \end{array}$$
$$\begin{array}{r} 81 \\ +18 \\ \hline \end{array}$$
$$\begin{array}{r} 77 \\ -33 \\ \hline \end{array}$$
$$\begin{array}{r} 94 \\ -54 \\ \hline \end{array}$$
$$\begin{array}{r} 14 \\ +13 \\ \hline \end{array}$$

2-Digit Subtraction without Regrouping

Solve each problem. Subtract the ones column first. Write the difference.

A.
$$\begin{array}{r} 24 \\ -\ 14 \\ \hline \end{array}$$
$$\begin{array}{r} 64 \\ -\ 24 \\ \hline \end{array}$$
$$\begin{array}{r} 83 \\ -\ 32 \\ \hline \end{array}$$
$$\begin{array}{r} 46 \\ -\ 15 \\ \hline \end{array}$$
$$\begin{array}{r} 87 \\ -\ 32 \\ \hline \end{array}$$

B.
$$\begin{array}{r} 98 \\ -\ 84 \\ \hline \end{array}$$
$$\begin{array}{r} 32 \\ -\ 12 \\ \hline \end{array}$$
$$\begin{array}{r} 57 \\ -\ 34 \\ \hline \end{array}$$
$$\begin{array}{r} 75 \\ -\ 62 \\ \hline \end{array}$$
$$\begin{array}{r} 29 \\ -\ 19 \\ \hline \end{array}$$

C.
$$\begin{array}{r} 59 \\ -\ 53 \\ \hline \end{array}$$
$$\begin{array}{r} 38 \\ -\ 22 \\ \hline \end{array}$$
$$\begin{array}{r} 80 \\ -\ 30 \\ \hline \end{array}$$
$$\begin{array}{r} 37 \\ -\ 14 \\ \hline \end{array}$$
$$\begin{array}{r} 66 \\ -\ 22 \\ \hline \end{array}$$

D.
$$\begin{array}{r} 50 \\ -\ 40 \\ \hline \end{array}$$
$$\begin{array}{r} 88 \\ -\ 44 \\ \hline \end{array}$$
$$\begin{array}{r} 99 \\ -\ 35 \\ \hline \end{array}$$
$$\begin{array}{r} 48 \\ -\ 26 \\ \hline \end{array}$$
$$\begin{array}{r} 62 \\ -\ 12 \\ \hline \end{array}$$

E.
$$\begin{array}{r} 38 \\ -\ 16 \\ \hline \end{array}$$
$$\begin{array}{r} 72 \\ -\ 32 \\ \hline \end{array}$$
$$\begin{array}{r} 96 \\ -\ 13 \\ \hline \end{array}$$
$$\begin{array}{r} 44 \\ -\ 12 \\ \hline \end{array}$$
$$\begin{array}{r} 65 \\ -\ 10 \\ \hline \end{array}$$

2-Digit Addition without Regrouping

Solve each problem. Add the ones column first. Write the sum.

A.
```
   78        26        75        24        34
 + 11      + 31      + 11      + 25      + 42
```

B.
```
   30        36        60        25        84
 + 10      + 42      + 20      + 41      + 12
```

C.
```
   24        31        74        55        45
 + 13      + 25      + 24      + 24      + 24
```

D.
```
   75        80        20        68        62
 + 24      + 10      + 10      + 11      + 31
```

E.
```
   43        66        54        82        53
 + 25      + 32      + 21      + 16      + 36
```

166

2-Digit Subtraction without Regrouping

Solve each problem. Subtract the ones column first. Write the difference.

A.
$$\begin{array}{r} 27 \\ -24 \\ \hline \end{array}$$
$$\begin{array}{r} 72 \\ -21 \\ \hline \end{array}$$
$$\begin{array}{r} 33 \\ -20 \\ \hline \end{array}$$
$$\begin{array}{r} 95 \\ -55 \\ \hline \end{array}$$
$$\begin{array}{r} 39 \\ -17 \\ \hline \end{array}$$

B.
$$\begin{array}{r} 39 \\ -38 \\ \hline \end{array}$$
$$\begin{array}{r} 50 \\ -40 \\ \hline \end{array}$$
$$\begin{array}{r} 77 \\ -25 \\ \hline \end{array}$$
$$\begin{array}{r} 81 \\ -30 \\ \hline \end{array}$$
$$\begin{array}{r} 28 \\ -12 \\ \hline \end{array}$$

C.
$$\begin{array}{r} 94 \\ -82 \\ \hline \end{array}$$
$$\begin{array}{r} 63 \\ -43 \\ \hline \end{array}$$
$$\begin{array}{r} 36 \\ -34 \\ \hline \end{array}$$
$$\begin{array}{r} 35 \\ -30 \\ \hline \end{array}$$
$$\begin{array}{r} 47 \\ -16 \\ \hline \end{array}$$

D.
$$\begin{array}{r} 81 \\ -41 \\ \hline \end{array}$$
$$\begin{array}{r} 25 \\ -24 \\ \hline \end{array}$$
$$\begin{array}{r} 55 \\ -40 \\ \hline \end{array}$$
$$\begin{array}{r} 82 \\ -10 \\ \hline \end{array}$$
$$\begin{array}{r} 69 \\ -24 \\ \hline \end{array}$$

E.
$$\begin{array}{r} 75 \\ -45 \\ \hline \end{array}$$
$$\begin{array}{r} 66 \\ -55 \\ \hline \end{array}$$
$$\begin{array}{r} 96 \\ -33 \\ \hline \end{array}$$
$$\begin{array}{r} 73 \\ -52 \\ \hline \end{array}$$
$$\begin{array}{r} 29 \\ -21 \\ \hline \end{array}$$

Writing Numbers: 400-449

Write the numbers to 449. Start at 400.

400									
					415				
	421								
				434					
						446			

Writing Numbers: 450-499

Write the numbers to 499. Start at 450.

450									
		462							
						476			
				495					

Writing Numbers: 400-499

Write the numbers to 499. Start at 400.

400									
		412							
									438
				454					
					466				
	481								
									499

Tens and Ones

Write how many tens and ones. Then, write the number.

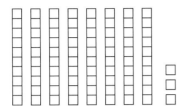

A. _____ tens _____ ones is the

same as _____

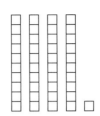

B. _____ tens _____ one is the

same as _____

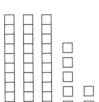

C. _____ tens _____ ones is the

same as _____

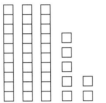

D. _____ tens _____ ones is the

same as _____

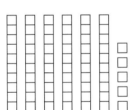

E. _____ tens _____ ones is the

same as _____

F. _____ ten _____ ones is the

same as _____

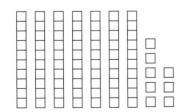

G. _____ tens _____ ones is the

same as _____

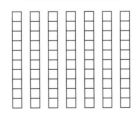

H. _____ tens _____ ones is the

same as _____

Hundreds, Tens, and Ones

Write how many hundreds, tens, and ones. Then, write the number.

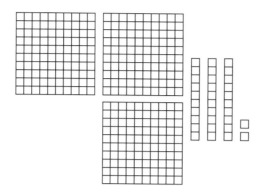

A. _____ hundreds _____ tens _____ ones is the same as _____

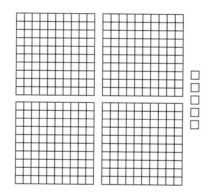

B. _____ hundreds _____ tens _____ ones is the same as _____

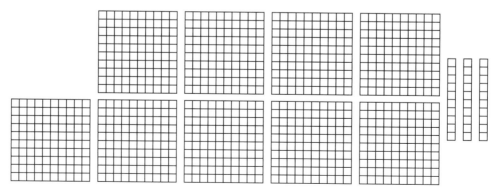

C. _____ hundreds _____ tens _____ ones is the same as _____

Hundreds, Tens, and Ones

Write how many hundreds, tens, and ones. Then, write the number.

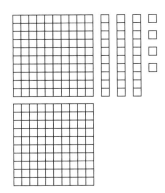

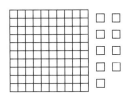

A. hundreds _____

    tens _____

    ones _____

    What number? _____

B. hundreds _____

    tens _____

    ones _____

    What number? _____

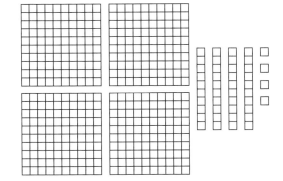

C. hundreds _____

    tens _____

    ones _____

    What number? _____

D. hundreds _____

    tens _____

    ones _____

    What number? _____

3-Digit Addition without Regrouping

Solve each problem. Add the ones column first. Write the sum.

A.
```
  614        730        212        723        500
+ 112      + 233      + 764      + 102      + 427
```

B.
```
  200        541        132        404        237
+ 300      + 136      + 121      + 171      + 131
```

C.
```
  541        851        584        422        247
+ 432      + 148      + 113      + 244      + 111
```

D.
```
  867        166        137        542        700
+ 102      + 312      + 621      + 321      + 200
```

E.
```
  226        524        446        604        131
+ 571      + 264      + 351      + 172      + 121
```

F.
```
  835        312        691        206        212
+ 142      + 446      + 107      + 102      + 313
```

3-Digit Subtraction without Regrouping

Solve each problem. Subtract the ones column first. Write the difference.

A.
$$\begin{array}{r} 864 \\ -123 \\ \hline \end{array}$$
$$\begin{array}{r} 286 \\ -133 \\ \hline \end{array}$$
$$\begin{array}{r} 648 \\ -141 \\ \hline \end{array}$$
$$\begin{array}{r} 984 \\ -400 \\ \hline \end{array}$$
$$\begin{array}{r} 748 \\ -124 \\ \hline \end{array}$$

B.
$$\begin{array}{r} 576 \\ -201 \\ \hline \end{array}$$
$$\begin{array}{r} 698 \\ -568 \\ \hline \end{array}$$
$$\begin{array}{r} 379 \\ -141 \\ \hline \end{array}$$
$$\begin{array}{r} 840 \\ -130 \\ \hline \end{array}$$
$$\begin{array}{r} 695 \\ -645 \\ \hline \end{array}$$

C.
$$\begin{array}{r} 327 \\ -213 \\ \hline \end{array}$$
$$\begin{array}{r} 762 \\ -241 \\ \hline \end{array}$$
$$\begin{array}{r} 844 \\ -523 \\ \hline \end{array}$$
$$\begin{array}{r} 539 \\ -425 \\ \hline \end{array}$$
$$\begin{array}{r} 775 \\ -225 \\ \hline \end{array}$$

D.
$$\begin{array}{r} 572 \\ -122 \\ \hline \end{array}$$
$$\begin{array}{r} 937 \\ -725 \\ \hline \end{array}$$
$$\begin{array}{r} 623 \\ -102 \\ \hline \end{array}$$
$$\begin{array}{r} 554 \\ -312 \\ \hline \end{array}$$
$$\begin{array}{r} 742 \\ -112 \\ \hline \end{array}$$

E.
$$\begin{array}{r} 245 \\ -124 \\ \hline \end{array}$$
$$\begin{array}{r} 667 \\ -324 \\ \hline \end{array}$$
$$\begin{array}{r} 263 \\ -152 \\ \hline \end{array}$$
$$\begin{array}{r} 614 \\ -313 \\ \hline \end{array}$$
$$\begin{array}{r} 867 \\ -120 \\ \hline \end{array}$$

F.
$$\begin{array}{r} 670 \\ -240 \\ \hline \end{array}$$
$$\begin{array}{r} 938 \\ -526 \\ \hline \end{array}$$
$$\begin{array}{r} 263 \\ -142 \\ \hline \end{array}$$
$$\begin{array}{r} 400 \\ -200 \\ \hline \end{array}$$
$$\begin{array}{r} 486 \\ -322 \\ \hline \end{array}$$

Word Problems

Write an addition or subtraction problem in the box for each story. Then, solve the problem and write the sum or difference on the line.

A. Jill and Ted work for Mr. Brown. One day, they picked apples for him. Jill picked 324 apples, and Ted picked 271. How many apples did they pick in all?

_____ apples in all

B. We went skiing last winter. The first day, we drove 223 miles, and on the second day, we drove 656 miles. How many more miles did we drive the second day?

_____ miles

C. There were 326 people in the theater on Friday. On Saturday, there were 214. How many more people were in the theater on Friday than on Saturday?

_____ more people on Friday

D. There were 845 people at the concert. At intermission, 325 left. How many people were left at the end of the concert?

_____ people

3-Digit Addition without Regrouping

Solve each problem. Add the ones column first. Write the sum.

A.
$$245 + 124$$ $$667 + 322$$ $$263 + 122$$ $$314 + 213$$ $$867 + 120$$

B.
$$376 + 522$$ $$212 + 701$$ $$777 + 222$$ $$306 + 103$$ $$220 + 346$$

C.
$$286 + 203$$ $$352 + 230$$ $$422 + 327$$ $$254 + 134$$ $$451 + 400$$

D.
$$486 + 302$$ $$522 + 371$$ $$570 + 223$$ $$368 + 120$$ $$279 + 100$$

3-Digit Subtraction without Regrouping

Solve each problem. Subtract the ones column first. Write the difference.

A.
$$684 - 343$$ $$723 - 520$$ $$325 - 113$$ $$467 - 251$$ $$214 - 112$$

B.
$$675 - 120$$ $$648 - 631$$ $$792 - 671$$ $$760 - 540$$ $$652 - 642$$

C.
$$227 - 113$$ $$557 - 326$$ $$819 - 705$$ $$548 - 136$$ $$784 - 252$$

D.
$$462 - 211$$ $$985 - 301$$ $$646 - 243$$ $$354 - 112$$ $$326 - 123$$

E.
$$750 - 350$$ $$642 - 131$$ $$379 - 161$$ $$846 - 631$$ $$527 - 215$$

Word Problems

Write a subtraction problem in the box for each story. Then, solve the problem and write the difference on the line.

A. We went on a trip last summer. The first day, we drove 241 miles, and on the second day, we drove 452 miles. How many more miles did we drive on the second day?

_____ miles

B. Mrs. Hill had 567 candles for sale in her store. By the end of the day, she had sold 325. How many candles did she have left?

_____ candles left

C. There were 160 people in the park on Monday. On Friday, there were 286. How many more people were in the park on Friday than on Monday?

_____ more people on Friday

D. There were 724 people at the ball game. When it began to rain, 510 left. How many people were left at the game?

_____ people

Writing Numbers: 500-549

Write the numbers to 549. Start at 500.

500									
						516			
		522							
					535				
							547		

Writing Numbers: 550-599

Write the numbers to 599. Start at 550.

550									
	561								
							577		
					585				
				594					

Writing Numbers: 500-599

Write the numbers to 599. Start at 500.

500									
	511								
									539
		553							
			565						
	581								
									599

Counting Coins

Count the coins in each row. Write the total amount on the line.

A. 25¢ + 25¢ + 25¢   = _____ ¢

B. 25¢ + 10¢ + 10¢ + 5¢   = _____ ¢

C. 25¢ + 5¢ + 5¢   = _____ ¢

D. 10¢ + 10¢ + 10¢ + 5¢   = _____ ¢

E. 25¢ + 25¢ + 1¢ + 1¢   = _____ ¢

Word Problems

Add the coins to solve each problem. Write the total amount on the line. Then, circle *yes* or *no* to answer the question.

A. Rick has 2 quarters and 1 dime.

   He has _____ ¢.

   Does he have enough money to buy a toy truck that costs 75¢?

   yes   no

B. Anna has 3 dimes and 4 nickels.

   She has_____¢.

   Does she have enough to buy a toy yo-yo that costs 25¢?

   yes   no

C. Mom gave Dianne 3 quarters and 2 dimes to buy milk.

   She has_____¢.

   The milk costs 92¢ per quart. Does she have enough to buy one quart

   of milk?   yes   no

D. Trent has 2 dimes, 1 nickel, and 4 pennies.

   He has _____¢.

   Does he have enough to buy a toy train that costs 46¢?

   yes   no

E. You have 1 half-dollar and 3 dimes.

   You have_____¢.

   Could you buy a kite that costs 95¢?

   yes   no

Word Problems

Add the coins to solve each problem. Write the total amount on the line. Then, circle *yes* or *no* to answer the question.

A.   Griffin has 8 nickels and 9 pennies.

   He has _____ ¢.

   Does he have enough to buy a notebook that costs 50¢?

   yes   no

B.   Randy has 4 quarters. He wants to buy a toy duck that costs 67¢.

   He has _____ ¢.

   Does he have enough to buy the duck?

   yes   no

C.   Lisa has 1 quarter, 2 dimes, 2 nickels, and 3 pennies.

   She has_____ ¢.

   She wants to buy a box of crayons that costs 75¢. Does she have enough to buy the crayons?   yes   no

D.   Dianne has 4 dimes, 2 nickels, and 7 pennies.

   She has_____ ¢.

   Does she have enough to buy a 50¢ storybook?

   yes   no

E.   Mike needs a new pen. The one he wants costs 35¢. He has 1 half-dollar.

   He has _____ ¢.

   Does he have enough to buy the pen?

   yes   no

Counting Coins

Count the coins in each row. Write the total amount on the line.

A. _____ ¢

B. _____ ¢

C. _____ ¢

D. _____ ¢

Counting Coins

Count the coins in each row. Write the total amount on the line.

A. _____ ¢

B. _____ ¢

C. _____ ¢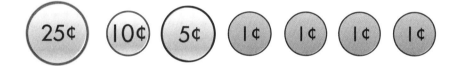

D. _____ ¢

Writing Numbers: 600-649

Write the numbers to 649. Start at 600.

600									
							617		
	621								
						636			
								648	

Writing Numbers: 650-699

Write the numbers to 699. Start at 650.

650									
		662							
								678	
				684					
					695				

Writing Numbers: 600-699

Write the numbers to 699. Start at 600.

600									
		612							
								638	
			654						
					667				
680									
									699

Identifying Fractions

Circle the fraction that tells how much is colored.

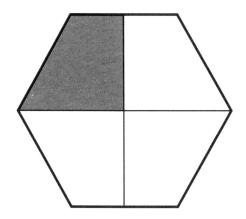

A. $\dfrac{1}{2}$ $\dfrac{1}{4}$ $\dfrac{1}{3}$ $\dfrac{2}{4}$

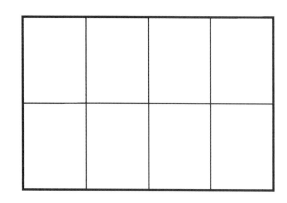

B. $\dfrac{3}{8}$ $\dfrac{5}{8}$ $\dfrac{1}{4}$ $\dfrac{5}{9}$

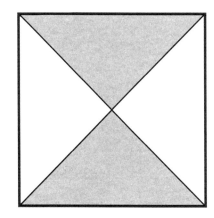

C. $\dfrac{2}{4}$ $\dfrac{3}{4}$ $\dfrac{1}{8}$ $\dfrac{1}{4}$

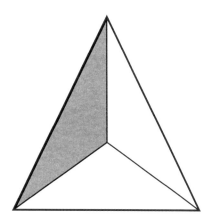

D. $\dfrac{1}{3}$ $\dfrac{2}{3}$ $\dfrac{3}{3}$ $\dfrac{2}{12}$

Writing Fractions

Write the fraction that tells how much is colored.

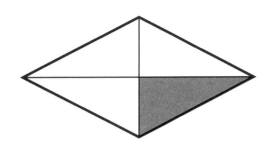

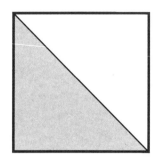

A. _____   B. _____

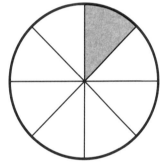

C. _____   D. _____

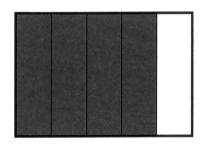

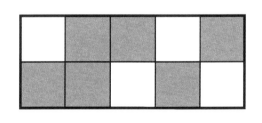

E. _____   F. _____

192

Writing Numbers: 700-749

Write the numbers to 749. Start at 700.

700									
					715				
							727		
	731								
				744					

Writing Numbers: 750-799

Write the numbers to 799. Start at 750.

750									
								768	
	771								
				785					
			794						

Writing Numbers: 700-799

Write the numbers to 799. Start at 700.

700									
				714					
									739
			753						
								768	
	781								
									799

2-Digit Addition with Regrouping

Solve each problem. Add the ones column first. Use the box to regroup and add the tens column. Write the sum.

A.
$$\begin{array}{r} \square \\ 58 \\ +\ 28 \\ \hline \end{array}$$
$$\begin{array}{r} \square \\ 41 \\ +\ 29 \\ \hline \end{array}$$
$$\begin{array}{r} \square \\ 66 \\ +\ 15 \\ \hline \end{array}$$
$$\begin{array}{r} \square \\ 45 \\ +\ 18 \\ \hline \end{array}$$
$$\begin{array}{r} \square \\ 17 \\ +\ 19 \\ \hline \end{array}$$

B.
$$\begin{array}{r} \square \\ 35 \\ +\ 27 \\ \hline \end{array}$$
$$\begin{array}{r} \square \\ 18 \\ +\ 23 \\ \hline \end{array}$$
$$\begin{array}{r} \square \\ 46 \\ +\ 14 \\ \hline \end{array}$$
$$\begin{array}{r} \square \\ 67 \\ +\ 25 \\ \hline \end{array}$$
$$\begin{array}{r} \square \\ 14 \\ +\ 19 \\ \hline \end{array}$$

C.
$$\begin{array}{r} \square \\ 68 \\ +\ 28 \\ \hline \end{array}$$
$$\begin{array}{r} \square \\ 47 \\ +\ 47 \\ \hline \end{array}$$
$$\begin{array}{r} \square \\ 65 \\ +\ 28 \\ \hline \end{array}$$
$$\begin{array}{r} \square \\ 16 \\ +\ 17 \\ \hline \end{array}$$
$$\begin{array}{r} \square \\ 56 \\ +\ 29 \\ \hline \end{array}$$

D.
$$\begin{array}{r} \square \\ 24 \\ +\ 18 \\ \hline \end{array}$$
$$\begin{array}{r} \square \\ 62 \\ +\ 18 \\ \hline \end{array}$$
$$\begin{array}{r} \square \\ 19 \\ +\ 32 \\ \hline \end{array}$$
$$\begin{array}{r} \square \\ 64 \\ +\ 37 \\ \hline \end{array}$$
$$\begin{array}{r} \square \\ 21 \\ +\ 79 \\ \hline \end{array}$$

2-Digit Addition with Regrouping

Solve each problem. Add the ones column first. Write the sum.

A.
$$\begin{array}{r} 13 \\ + 29 \\ \hline \end{array} \qquad \begin{array}{r} 33 \\ + 59 \\ \hline \end{array} \qquad \begin{array}{r} 58 \\ + 28 \\ \hline \end{array} \qquad \begin{array}{r} 25 \\ + 25 \\ \hline \end{array} \qquad \begin{array}{r} 28 \\ + 29 \\ \hline \end{array}$$

B.
$$\begin{array}{r} 17 \\ + 33 \\ \hline \end{array} \qquad \begin{array}{r} 74 \\ + 77 \\ \hline \end{array} \qquad \begin{array}{r} 43 \\ + 39 \\ \hline \end{array} \qquad \begin{array}{r} 68 \\ + 27 \\ \hline \end{array} \qquad \begin{array}{r} 67 \\ + 69 \\ \hline \end{array}$$

C.
$$\begin{array}{r} 44 \\ + 49 \\ \hline \end{array} \qquad \begin{array}{r} 18 \\ + 19 \\ \hline \end{array} \qquad \begin{array}{r} 48 \\ + 58 \\ \hline \end{array} \qquad \begin{array}{r} 55 \\ + 66 \\ \hline \end{array} \qquad \begin{array}{r} 55 \\ + 45 \\ \hline \end{array}$$

D.
$$\begin{array}{r} 94 \\ + 17 \\ \hline \end{array} \qquad \begin{array}{r} 77 \\ + 66 \\ \hline \end{array} \qquad \begin{array}{r} 67 \\ + 67 \\ \hline \end{array} \qquad \begin{array}{r} 92 \\ + 29 \\ \hline \end{array} \qquad \begin{array}{r} 57 \\ + 47 \\ \hline \end{array}$$

E.
$$\begin{array}{r} 63 \\ + 27 \\ \hline \end{array} \qquad \begin{array}{r} 35 \\ + 17 \\ \hline \end{array} \qquad \begin{array}{r} 41 \\ + 29 \\ \hline \end{array} \qquad \begin{array}{r} 25 \\ + 46 \\ \hline \end{array} \qquad \begin{array}{r} 45 \\ + 58 \\ \hline \end{array}$$

F.
$$\begin{array}{r} 66 \\ + 57 \\ \hline \end{array} \qquad \begin{array}{r} 11 \\ + 59 \\ \hline \end{array} \qquad \begin{array}{r} 43 \\ + 87 \\ \hline \end{array} \qquad \begin{array}{r} 47 \\ + 83 \\ \hline \end{array} \qquad \begin{array}{r} 15 \\ + 98 \\ \hline \end{array}$$

2-Digit Addition

Solve each problem. Add the ones column first. Regroup if needed.
Write the sum.

A.
$$36 + 17$$
$$33 + 14$$
$$51 + 34$$
$$53 + 24$$
$$84 + 27$$

B.
$$85 + 26$$
$$64 + 18$$
$$67 + 29$$
$$30 + 18$$
$$34 + 17$$

C.
$$61 + 32$$
$$43 + 34$$
$$20 + 12$$
$$35 + 16$$
$$43 + 28$$

D.
$$83 + 55$$
$$52 + 35$$
$$63 + 26$$
$$77 + 38$$
$$66 + 48$$

E.
$$65 + 17$$
$$31 + 24$$
$$52 + 14$$
$$78 + 29$$
$$83 + 26$$

2-Digit Addition

Solve each problem. Add the ones column first. Regroup if needed. Write the sum.

A.
$$68 + 23$$
$$50 + 13$$
$$52 + 13$$
$$72 + 14$$
$$31 + 18$$

B.
$$47 + 29$$
$$43 + 31$$
$$71 + 35$$
$$90 + 55$$
$$61 + 19$$

C.
$$58 + 29$$
$$32 + 13$$
$$82 + 36$$
$$81 + 28$$
$$33 + 15$$

D.
$$50 + 35$$
$$77 + 39$$
$$91 + 34$$
$$20 + 32$$
$$52 + 24$$

E.
$$26 + 18$$
$$53 + 36$$
$$42 + 37$$
$$44 + 25$$
$$17 + 14$$

2-Digit Addition

Solve each problem. Add the ones column first. Regroup if needed. Write the sum.

A.
$$48 + 28$$
$$32 + 13$$
$$16 + 19$$
$$57 + 45$$
$$61 + 28$$

B.
$$95 + 27$$
$$67 + 27$$
$$47 + 19$$
$$51 + 33$$
$$93 + 46$$

C.
$$24 + 15$$
$$60 + 37$$
$$36 + 13$$
$$57 + 28$$
$$25 + 15$$

D.
$$60 + 42$$
$$88 + 46$$
$$65 + 48$$
$$46 + 32$$
$$21 + 15$$

E.
$$55 + 15$$
$$67 + 27$$
$$82 + 16$$
$$48 + 17$$
$$22 + 17$$

2-Digit Addition

Solve each problem. Regroup if needed. Write the sum on the line.

A. 54 + 19 = _____

  51 + 38 = _____

  62 + 30 = _____

  43 + 26 = _____

  26 + 13 = _____

  44 + 40 = _____

B. 15 + 12 = _____

  59 + 56 = _____

  21 + 18 = _____

  38 + 35 = _____

  45 + 42 = _____

  18 + 19 = _____

C. 75 + 33 = _____

  71 + 23 = _____

  90 + 50 = _____

  77 + 57 = _____

  38 + 24 = _____

  87 + 45 = _____

D. 94 + 18 = _____

  49 + 24 = _____

  38 + 13 = _____

  82 + 47 = _____

  52 + 27 = _____

  67 + 42 = _____

Number Puzzle

Read and solve each clue. Then, complete the puzzle (page 203) by writing the answers in the correct spaces.

Across

1. $84 + 33 =$ _____
2. $28 - 12 =$ _____
4. $95 + 13 =$ _____
5. $90 + 10 =$ _____
6. 10 more than 60 is _____
7. $924 + 123 =$ _____
9. 1 less than 14 is _____
10. the number after fifty-six is _____
11. 15 more than 30 is _____
12. $316 + 282 =$ _____
13. when counting by 2s, this number comes after 84 _____
15. the number after 99 is _____

Down

1. $67 + 48 =$ _____
2. 2 more than 126 is _____
3. $94 + 26 =$ _____
4. 1 less than 13 is _____
7. $84 - 71 =$ _____
8. 2 hundreds, 8 tens, 4 ones _____
12. $210 + 321 =$ _____
13. 10 less than 96 is _____
14. $29 - 16 =$ _____

202

Number Puzzle

Use the answers (page 202) to complete the puzzle.

Column Addition with Regrouping

Solve each problem. Add the ones column first. Write the sum.

A.
```
    50        13        20        62        23
    12        46        48        66        15
  + 19      + 73      + 39      + 84      + 14
```

B.
```
    25        18        19        17        11
    35        31        14        33        48
  + 45      + 62      +  7      + 43      + 24
```

C.
```
    62        13        60        31        23
     7        16        78        28        42
  +  5      + 14      +  8      + 35      + 16
```

D.
```
    51        33        32        43        68
    33        66        66        95        54
  + 19      + 44      + 46      + 46      + 62
```

E.
```
    37        30        48        12        38
    40        19        27         5        56
  + 26      +  5      + 15      +  8      + 63
```

Word Problems

Write an addition problem in the box for each story. Then, solve each problem and write the sum.

A. There were 16 people walking in the park and 28 people jogging. How many people were at the park in all?

B. Julie's mother planted 88 tulip bulbs and 19 daffodil bulbs. How many bulbs did she plant in all?

C. Kirk had two bags of peanuts. One bag had 24 peanuts and the other bag had 69. How many total peanuts did Kirk have?

D. Amy Marie has 49¢. She found a quarter. How much money does she have?

E. Cindy sold 47 CDs on Monday and 15 CDs on Tuesday. How many CDs did she sell in all?

3-Digit Addition with Regrouping

Solve each problem. Add the ones column first. Use the boxes to regroup. Write the sum.

A.
$\square$
245
+ 129

$\square$
552
+ 164

$\square\square$
368
+ 167

$\square$
163
+ 329

$\square$
472
+ 518

B.
$\square$
146
+ 693

$\square$
458
+ 227

$\square$
173
+ 281

$\square$
239
+ 126

$\square$
824
+ 129

C.
$\square$
180
+ 350

$\square$
564
+ 338

$\square$
439
+ 127

$\square$
374
+ 217

$\square$
640
+ 196

D.
$\square$
575
+ 119

$\square$
136
+ 129

$\square$
605
+ 266

$\square$
276
+ 407

$\square$
498
+ 141

E.
$\square$
224
+ 538

$\square\square$
569
+ 146

$\square$
267
+ 181

$\square\square$
129
+ 189

$\square$
278
+ 261

Adding Money

Solve each problem. Add the ones column first. Regroup if needed. Write the sum. Add the decimal point and dollar sign to your answer. The first problem has been done for you.

A. $1.10 $3.84 $1.26 $1.21 $1.32
  + $2.20   + $1.14   + $2.01   + $0.67   + $0.41
   $3.30

B. $4.65 $2.81 $6.19 $3.04 $8.16
  + $1.22   + $1.08   + $2.40   + $1.02   + $1.22

C. $6.29 $1.88 $4.66 $2.22 $5.50
  + $1.27   + $2.16   + $1.29   + $2.48   + $2.17

D. $2.25 $6.41 $9.75 $3.33 $1.29
  + $1.28   + $1.58   + $0.15   + $1.58   + $1.39

3-Digit Addition

Solve each problem. Add the ones column first. Regroup if needed.
Write the sum.

A.
$$875 + 406$$
$$141 + 157$$
$$843 + 327$$
$$648 + 252$$
$$286 + 137$$

B.
$$984 + 296$$
$$885 + 147$$
$$671 + 366$$
$$352 + 204$$
$$622 + 144$$

C.
$$142 + 136$$
$$328 + 182$$
$$555 + 388$$
$$210 + 197$$
$$332 + 146$$

D.
$$300 + 132$$
$$379 + 289$$
$$521 + 139$$
$$110 + 179$$
$$213 + 142$$

E.
$$216 + 139$$
$$777 + 532$$
$$824 + 157$$
$$319 + 216$$
$$469 + 122$$

Writing Numbers: 800-849

Write the numbers to 849. Start at 800.

800									
							817		
	821								
						836			
								848	

Writing Numbers: 850-899

Write the numbers to 899. Start at 850.

850									
		862							
								878	
				884					
					895				

Writing Numbers: 800-899

Write the numbers to 899. Start at 800.

800									
					815				
			833						
							857		
	862								
								888	
									899

2-Digit Subtraction with Regrouping

Solve each problem. Subtract the ones column first. Write the difference.

A.
$$\begin{array}{r} 61 \\ -\ 28 \\ \hline \end{array}$$
$$\begin{array}{r} 60 \\ -\ 12 \\ \hline \end{array}$$
$$\begin{array}{r} 72 \\ -\ 19 \\ \hline \end{array}$$
$$\begin{array}{r} 95 \\ -\ 26 \\ \hline \end{array}$$
$$\begin{array}{r} 74 \\ -\ 58 \\ \hline \end{array}$$

B.
$$\begin{array}{r} 44 \\ -\ 16 \\ \hline \end{array}$$
$$\begin{array}{r} 52 \\ -\ 29 \\ \hline \end{array}$$
$$\begin{array}{r} 73 \\ -\ 19 \\ \hline \end{array}$$
$$\begin{array}{r} 67 \\ -\ 28 \\ \hline \end{array}$$
$$\begin{array}{r} 45 \\ -\ 27 \\ \hline \end{array}$$

C.
$$\begin{array}{r} 36 \\ -\ 17 \\ \hline \end{array}$$
$$\begin{array}{r} 33 \\ -\ 14 \\ \hline \end{array}$$
$$\begin{array}{r} 51 \\ -\ 34 \\ \hline \end{array}$$
$$\begin{array}{r} 53 \\ -\ 24 \\ \hline \end{array}$$
$$\begin{array}{r} 84 \\ -\ 27 \\ \hline \end{array}$$

D.
$$\begin{array}{r} 85 \\ -\ 26 \\ \hline \end{array}$$
$$\begin{array}{r} 64 \\ -\ 18 \\ \hline \end{array}$$
$$\begin{array}{r} 67 \\ -\ 29 \\ \hline \end{array}$$
$$\begin{array}{r} 30 \\ -\ 18 \\ \hline \end{array}$$
$$\begin{array}{r} 34 \\ -\ 17 \\ \hline \end{array}$$

E.
$$\begin{array}{r} 32 \\ -\ 14 \\ \hline \end{array}$$
$$\begin{array}{r} 50 \\ -\ 18 \\ \hline \end{array}$$
$$\begin{array}{r} 28 \\ -\ 19 \\ \hline \end{array}$$
$$\begin{array}{r} 42 \\ -\ 28 \\ \hline \end{array}$$
$$\begin{array}{r} 84 \\ -\ 19 \\ \hline \end{array}$$

Addition and Subtraction Wheel

Solve each problem. Add or subtract in order. Write the answers around the wheel to reach the center.

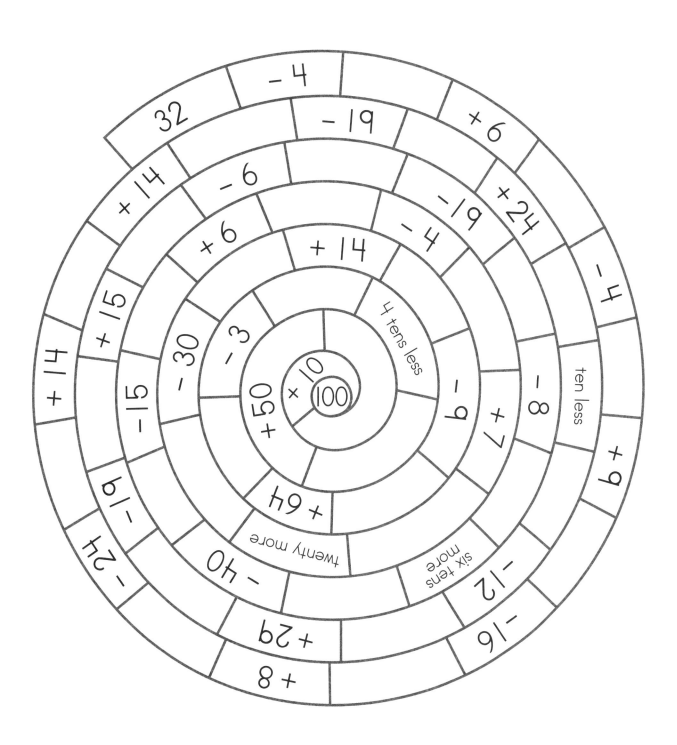

2-Digit Subtraction

Solve each problem. Subtract the ones column first. Regroup if needed.
Write the difference.

A.
$$92 - 56$$ $$48 - 21$$ $$82 - 46$$ $$46 - 10$$ $$79 - 43$$

B.
$$47 - 28$$ $$61 - 42$$ $$58 - 39$$ $$33 - 14$$ $$72 - 14$$

C.
$$39 - 27$$ $$47 - 44$$ $$50 - 38$$ $$22 - 11$$ $$24 - 12$$

D.
$$54 - 19$$ $$51 - 38$$ $$62 - 30$$ $$43 - 26$$ $$44 - 40$$

E.
$$84 - 32$$ $$45 - 35$$ $$98 - 46$$ $$65 - 54$$ $$81 - 16$$

2-Digit Subtraction

Solve each problem. Subtract the ones column first. Regroup if needed.
Write the difference.

A.
$$96 - 28$$ $$84 - 39$$ $$47 - 18$$ $$64 - 47$$ $$82 - 68$$

B.
$$95 - 47$$ $$34 - 29$$ $$24 - 10$$ $$26 - 15$$ $$31 - 17$$

C.
$$62 - 36$$ $$85 - 46$$ $$74 - 28$$ $$82 - 18$$ $$80 - 18$$

D.
$$75 - 38$$ $$56 - 49$$ $$65 - 16$$ $$38 - 29$$ $$42 - 28$$

E.
$$51 - 42$$ $$45 - 26$$ $$71 - 12$$ $$82 - 16$$ $$48 - 16$$

2-Digit Subtraction

**Solve each problem. Subtract the ones column first. Regroup if needed.
Write the difference.**

A.
$$\begin{array}{r} 34 \\ -18 \\ \hline \end{array}$$
$$\begin{array}{r} 51 \\ -38 \\ \hline \end{array}$$
$$\begin{array}{r} 42 \\ -16 \\ \hline \end{array}$$
$$\begin{array}{r} 38 \\ -22 \\ \hline \end{array}$$
$$\begin{array}{r} 49 \\ -28 \\ \hline \end{array}$$

B.
$$\begin{array}{r} 25 \\ -13 \\ \hline \end{array}$$
$$\begin{array}{r} 30 \\ -19 \\ \hline \end{array}$$
$$\begin{array}{r} 56 \\ -42 \\ \hline \end{array}$$
$$\begin{array}{r} 83 \\ -38 \\ \hline \end{array}$$
$$\begin{array}{r} 77 \\ -44 \\ \hline \end{array}$$

C.
$$\begin{array}{r} 26 \\ -18 \\ \hline \end{array}$$
$$\begin{array}{r} 33 \\ -30 \\ \hline \end{array}$$
$$\begin{array}{r} 88 \\ -38 \\ \hline \end{array}$$
$$\begin{array}{r} 64 \\ -25 \\ \hline \end{array}$$
$$\begin{array}{r} 23 \\ -20 \\ \hline \end{array}$$

D.
$$\begin{array}{r} 44 \\ -26 \\ \hline \end{array}$$
$$\begin{array}{r} 75 \\ -67 \\ \hline \end{array}$$
$$\begin{array}{r} 23 \\ -13 \\ \hline \end{array}$$
$$\begin{array}{r} 67 \\ -39 \\ \hline \end{array}$$
$$\begin{array}{r} 84 \\ -15 \\ \hline \end{array}$$

E.
$$\begin{array}{r} 63 \\ -47 \\ \hline \end{array}$$
$$\begin{array}{r} 24 \\ -14 \\ \hline \end{array}$$
$$\begin{array}{r} 37 \\ -19 \\ \hline \end{array}$$
$$\begin{array}{r} 76 \\ -17 \\ \hline \end{array}$$
$$\begin{array}{r} 54 \\ -18 \\ \hline \end{array}$$

Subtraction

Solve each problem. Regroup if needed. Write the difference on the line.

A. $24 - 12 =$ _____

$39 - 27 =$ _____

$16 - 12 =$ _____

$47 - 44 =$ _____

$50 - 38 =$ _____

$22 - 11 =$ _____

B. $42 - 16 =$ _____

$94 - 68 =$ _____

$32 - 14 =$ _____

$17 - 16 =$ _____

$87 - 61 =$ _____

$36 - 10 =$ _____

C. $67 - 29 =$ _____

$21 - 9 =$ _____

$43 - 26 =$ _____

$55 - 38 =$ _____

$72 - 14 =$ _____

$33 - 16 =$ _____

D. $44 - 19 =$ _____

$32 - 11 =$ _____

$61 - 31 =$ _____

$24 - 22 =$ _____

$55 - 25 =$ _____

$48 - 18 =$ _____

Word Problems

Write a subtraction problem in the box for each story. Then, solve each problem and write the difference.

A. We put 42 cans of fruit on the shelf. A woman bought 14 of them. How many cans of fruit are left on the shelf?

B. Stacy's box of animal crackers has 41 crackers. Jamal's box has 67. How many more animal crackers does Jamal have?

C. I lined up 52 dominoes. Fourteen of them did not fall over. How many dominoes did fall?

D. Yolanda is going on vacation for 21 days this year. Last year she went for 18 days. How many more days will she be on vacation this year than last year?

Word Problems

Write a subtraction problem in the box for each story. Then, solve each problem and write the difference.

A. We counted 84 peaches on our tree. Some fell off. There are still 68 peaches on the tree. How many peaches fell off?

B. My friend and I tried to guess how many jelly beans were in a bag at the store. I guessed 48, and my friend guessed 97. How many more jelly beans did she guess?

C. Anna collected 78 bottle caps. Rex collected 29 fewer than Anna. How many bottle caps did Rex collect?

D. After school on Tuesday, 86 children went swimming. Nineteen of them left before the others. How many children were left in the pool?

Word Problems

Write an addition or subtraction problem for each story. Then, solve each problem and write the sum or difference.

A. In the forest, there are 92 deer. If 25 deer ran out of the forest, how many are still in the forest?

B. We counted 76 apples on our tree. Some fell off. There are still 59 apples on the tree. How many apples fell off?

C. My friend and I guessed how many buttons fell on the floor. I guessed 16, and my friend guessed 42. How many more buttons did she guess?

D. Megan collected 81 rocks. Alec collected 18 more than Megan. How many rocks did Alec collect?

E. After school on Friday, 31 children played softball. Thirteen of them left before the others. How many children were left playing?

3-Digit Subtraction with Regrouping

Solve each problem. Subtract the ones column first. Write the difference.

A.
```
  624        362        609        378        809
- 135      - 213      - 319      - 179      - 512
```

B.
```
  564        950        369        460        648
- 377      - 108      - 194      - 278      - 129
```

C.
```
  528        437        644        434        942
- 134      - 129      - 246      - 225      - 367
```

D.
```
  410        940        864        717        547
- 132      - 138      - 239      - 226      - 139
```

E.
```
  236        333        519        933        296
- 129      - 224      - 287      - 140      - 137
```

3-Digit Subtraction

Solve each problem. Subtract the ones column first. Regroup if needed.
Write the difference.

A.
$$368 - 229$$ $$422 - 145$$ $$422 - 312$$ $$325 - 132$$ $$745 - 146$$

B.
$$509 - 498$$ $$229 - 149$$ $$670 - 384$$ $$639 - 327$$ $$729 - 630$$

C.
$$243 - 138$$ $$511 - 462$$ $$775 - 187$$ $$622 - 219$$ $$330 - 129$$

D.
$$948 - 848$$ $$394 - 139$$ $$427 - 272$$ $$136 - 134$$ $$796 - 598$$

E.
$$480 - 246$$ $$347 - 264$$ $$336 - 136$$ $$126 - 113$$ $$648 - 154$$

Writing Numbers: 900-949

Write the numbers to 949. Start at 900.

900									
						916			
		922							
					935				
			943						

Writing Numbers: 950–999

Write the numbers to 999. Start at 950.

950									
			963						
				974					
					985				
								998	

Writing Numbers: 900-999

Write the numbers to 999. Start at 900.

900									
							927		
	931								
								958	
		963							
						986			
									999

Challenge: Time Will Tell

Look at each clock. Write the time two ways.

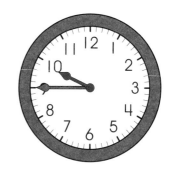

A. _____ or _____ minutes

after _____ o'clock

B. _____ or _____ minutes

after _____ o'clock

C. _____ or _____ minutes

after _____ o'clock

D. _____ or _____ minutes

after _____ o'clock

Read the story. Show the correct time on each clock. Then, write the time.

E. Starting at 12:10, Anna needs to call her mother every two hours. At what times should Anna call?

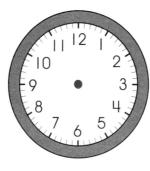

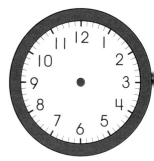

12:10 _____   _____   _____

Challenge: Signs and Patterns

Put a (+) or (–) in each box to solve the problem.

A. 6 ☐ 4 = 10

B. 2 ☐ 8 = 10

C. 10 ☐ 2 = 12

D. 7 ☐ 3 = 10

E. 7 ☐ 5 = 2

F. 4 ☐ 5 = 9

G. 9 ☐ 7 = 2

H. 9 ☐ 3 = 6

Finish each pattern.

I. F J O Y F J O Y F ____ ____ ____

J. ☺ ☺ ☺ ☺ ☹ ☹ ☺ ____ ____ ____ ____ ____

K. 1 3 8 6 2 4 9 1 3 ____ ____ ____ ____ ____

Challenge: Silly Sleuthing

Someone has secretly eaten the pie that everyone was going to share after dinner! Solve each problem. Then, circle the matching answers (page 229) to find out who did it.

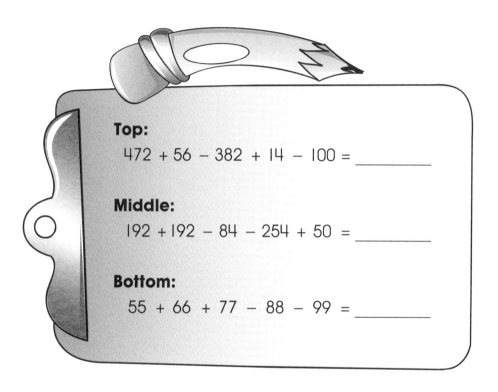

Top:

$$472 + 56 - 382 + 14 - 100 = \underline{\hspace{2cm}}$$

Middle:

$$192 + 192 - 84 - 254 + 50 = \underline{\hspace{2cm}}$$

Bottom:

$$55 + 66 + 77 - 88 - 99 = \underline{\hspace{2cm}}$$

Jordan   Lynn   Austin

Challenge: Silly Sleuthing

Find out what the suspect looks like. Circle your answers to match the suspect to the clues.

Top:

12   72   60

Middle:

57   96   103

Bottom:

11   17   2

Who ate the pie? _____

Challenge: Octopus Math

Solve each problem on the octopus. Then, answer each question.

On the octopus tentacles:

- $5 + 10 = $ _____
- $____ + 15 = $ _____
- $7 + 10 = $ _____
- $____ + 10 = $ _____
- $____ - 7 = $ _____
- $12 - 2 = $ _____
- $____ + 20 = $ _____
- $20 + 1 = $ _____
- $____ + 9 = $ _____
- $7 - 5 = $ _____
- $____ + 15 = $ _____
- $15 + 15 = $ _____
- $20 - 10 = $ _____
- $____ + 3 = $ _____
- $____ + 10 = $ _____

A. How many tentacles have the answer 30? _____

B. How many tentacles have the answer 20? _____

Challenge: Candy, Candy

Read the story. Then, answer each question.

Hudson bought 10 pieces of candy. On the way to Maddie's house, Hudson ate all but 4 pieces. If he shares half of what is left with Maddie . . .

A.   How many pieces of candy will Maddie have? _____

B.   How many pieces of candy will Hudson eat in all? _____

Challenge: Dot-to-Dot

Count backward by 5s to connect the dots. Start at 100 and end at 0.

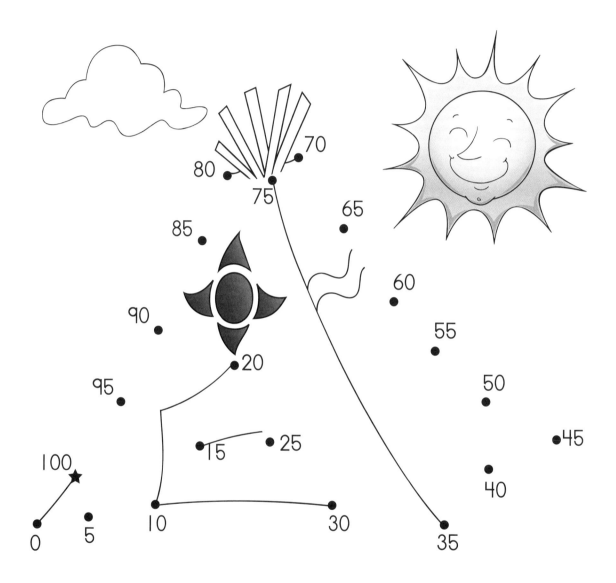

Challenge: Money Math

Read the story. Look at the picture. Use addition and subtraction to answer each question. Then, circle the pets that no one adopted.

Lisa, Dianne, and Mike went to the animal shelter. They each had $5.00 to adopt a pet. Lisa adopted 2 goldfish. Dianne adopted a puppy. Mike adopted a kitten. How much money did each of them have left?

Lisa had $ _____ left.

Dianne had $ _____ left.

Mike had $ _____ left.

Who had the most money left? _____

Puppies $2.50 each

Kittens $3.00 each

Fish $1.00 each

Challenge: Telling Time

Look at each clock. Write the time two ways.

A. _____ or _____ minutes

after _____ o'clock

B. _____ or _____ minutes

after _____ o'clock

C. _____ or _____ minutes

after _____ o'clock

D. _____ or _____ minutes

after _____ o'clock

Challenge: Picture Problems

How many peanuts did the elephant eat? Solve each problem to find the answer. Then, circle the peanut with the correct number.

92 - 16 = ____ - 27 = ____ - 15 = ____ - 4 = ____ - 15 =

15

13

17

32

12

20

27

Challenge: Greater Than or Less Than

Write a greater than (>) or less than (<) sign on each line to complete the comparison. The first problem has been done for you.

A. 14 __<__ 19

    16 _____ 17

    12 _____ 8

    17 _____ 18

B. 10 _____ 9

    11 _____ 6

    0 _____ 1

    15 _____ 7

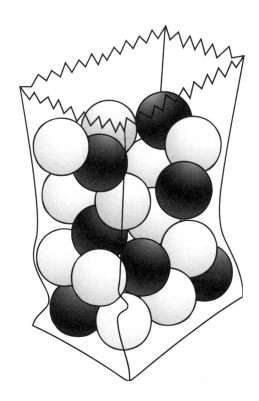

Read the story. Then, answer the question on the lines.

The bag above has black and white marbles in it. Look closely at the marbles. If you reached into the bag and took a handful, do you think that you would have more black marbles or more white marbles? Why?

I would have more _____ marbles.

_____

_____

236

Challenge: Popcorn Problems

Solve each problem. Write the difference. Circle each kernel whose difference is an odd number.

I. 47
  − 13

J. 27
  − 13

A. 59
  − 17

H. 89
  − 9

G. 12
  − 12

B.   7
  − 2

F. 59
  − 13

C. 26
  − 4

D. 16
  − 7

E. 67
  − 7

Challenge: Crossword Puzzle

Read and solve each clue. Choose a word from the Word Bank to answer each question. Complete the puzzle (page 239).

Word Bank

three	two	eleven	equation	clock	solve
nine	subtraction	sixteen	number	school	hands

Across

1. 17 – 14 = _____

4. Kids go to _____ to learn.

6. The opposite of addition is _____.

9. Numbers and symbols like 5 – 3 = 2 are called an _____.

10. 56 – 47 = _____

11. To find the answer is to _____ the equation.

Down

1. You have _____ eyes.

2. The number of months in a year minus one is _____.

3. 27 – 11 = _____

5. A _____ is something that tells time.

7. Nine is an odd _____ .

8. The _____ on a clock tell you what time it is.

Challenge: Crossword Puzzle

Challenge: Profit or Not?

Read the story. Then, answer the question.

Marcus bought a baseball card for $15. Trent saw the card and paid Marcus $20 for it. A few weeks later, Marcus wanted the baseball card back, so he paid Trent $25 for it. Then, Marcus sold the card to Rick for $30.

How much money did Marcus make? _____

Challenge: Addition Riddle

Solve each problem. Write the sum. Match the sums to the numbers below.
Then, write the letters on the lines to solve the riddle.

$$\begin{array}{r} 245 \\ + 429 \\ \hline \end{array}\ R \qquad \begin{array}{r} 617 \\ + 306 \\ \hline \end{array}\ E \qquad \begin{array}{r} 532 \\ + 428 \\ \hline \end{array}\ K \qquad \begin{array}{r} 546 \\ + 29 \\ \hline \end{array}\ B$$

$$\begin{array}{r} 385 \\ + 107 \\ \hline \end{array}\ H \qquad \begin{array}{r} 218 \\ + 145 \\ \hline \end{array}\ I \qquad \begin{array}{r} 439 \\ + 449 \\ \hline \end{array}\ Y \qquad \begin{array}{r} 374 \\ + 206 \\ \hline \end{array}\ D$$

$$\begin{array}{r} 708 \\ + 59 \\ \hline \end{array}\ C \qquad \begin{array}{r} 274 \\ + 316 \\ \hline \end{array}\ A \qquad \begin{array}{r} 137 \\ + 507 \\ \hline \end{array}\ T$$

What kind of cake likes to party?

____ ____ ____ ____ ____ ____ ____ ____ ____
590   575   363   674   644   492   580   590   888

____ ____ ____ ____!
767   590   960   923

Answer Key

Page 6
1. dog; 2. house; 3. gate; 4. tent;
5. bike; 6. deer

Page 7
1. corn; 2. bed; 3. book; 4. cat;
5. leaf; 6. drum

Page 8
1. b; 2. t; 3. l; 4. p; 5. d; 6. p; 7. r; 8. t

Page 9
1. pat, mat, fat; 2. ram, ham, Pam;
3. tap, map, cap; 4. ax, wax, tax;
5. bad, mad, had; 6. dad, pad, lad

Page 10
web, bed, jet, tent, vet

Page 11
1. fish; 2. sink; 3. six; 4. swim; 5. wish

Page 12
1. hot, dog; 2. frog, pond; 3. Mom, on,
log; 4. rock, hot; 5. drop, pot; 6. Tom, lot,
of, socks; 7. lock, box; 8. doll, mop; 9. fox,
loves, box; 10. Bobby, collects, rocks

Page 13
Answers will vary.

Page 14
1. cake; 2. rain; 3. pail; 4. plate

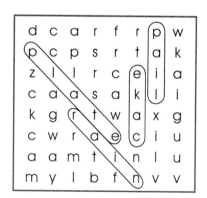

Page 15
week, sea, beak, feet, eat, tree

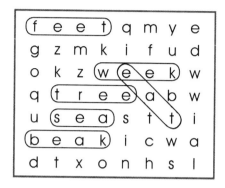

Page 16
1. bike; 2. fly; 3. line; 4. side; 5. mile;
Sentences will vary.

Page 17
1. road; 2. soap; 3. toad; 4. coat;
5. note; 6. bone

Page 18
1. flute; 2. music; 3. tube; 4. bugle

Page 19
1. baseball; 2. peanut; 3. oatmeal;
4. cupcake; 5. rainbow; 6. bedtime;
7.–12. Order of words will vary, but words
should be spelled correctly.

Page 20
Across: 2. anthill; 3. popcorn; 6. pancake;
7. mailbox; 8. sandbox; Down:
1. backpack; 4. raincoat; 5. sailboat

Page 21

Answer Key

Page 22
I. open; 2. boxes; 3. inside; 4. puppet;
5. mitten; 6. wagons

Page 23
I. candle; 2. whistle; 3. puddle;
4. giggle; 5. apple; 6. bubble

Page 24
I. B.; 2. D.; 3. C.; 4. A.

Page 25
I. city; 2. cat; 3. cell; 4. cent; *City, cell,*
and *cent* should be circled in yellow.
Cat should be circled in red.

Page 26
Carrie: carrot, cone, cane, camel, case;
Cecil: circle, cereal, center, cellar,
celery

Page 27
I. hard; 2. soft; 3. soft; 4. soft; 5. hard;
6. soft; 7. hard; 8. hard; 9. soft; IO. soft;
II. soft; I2. soft

Page 28
Soft g words: giraffe, gerbil, gem, germ,
gym, giant, gel, genius, George, general,
gentle, gypsy, genie, gentleman, ginger;
Hard g words: gate, goat, gopher, guitar,
gone, good, gold, gown, goal, gaze, gill,
gutter, game, gap, gum

Page 29
I. gate; 2. nice; 3. grew; 4. table

Page 30
I. bread; 2. branch; 3. grass; 4. fruit;
5. truck; 6. drum; 7. price; 8. frog; 9. tree

Page 31
I. glue, glass; 2. flat, flag; 3. clock, class;
4. plant, plane, 5. blow, blue; 6. slow, slick

Page 32
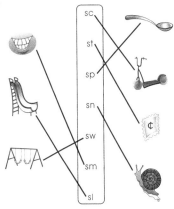

Page 33
I. camp; 2. stump; 3. tent; 4. trunk;
5. raft

Page 34
I. body; 2. daddy; 3. shy; 4. try; 5. tiny;
6. funny

Page 35
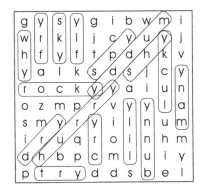

Page 36
I. dress; 2. trunk; 3. Try; 4. stuck;
5. scream; 6. sneaky

Page 37
peach: each, beach; shirt: shake, shoe;
whale: wheel, white; thirty: thin, this

Page 38
I. shop; 2. chair; 3. lunch; 4. choose;
5. what; 6. peach

Answer Key

Page 39
1. this; 2. with; 3. peach; 4. cash; 5. dish; 6. why; 7. write; 8. teeth

Page 40
1. kneel; 2. know; 3. knock; 4. knot; 5. knight; 6. knee

Page 41
1. wreath; 2. wrap; 3. wrinkles; 4. wrench; 5. wrist; 6. wren

Page 42

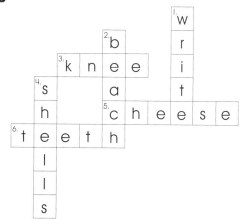

Page 43
hard: yard, lard, card; cart: smart, part, dart; shark: lark, dark, park

Page 44
1. born; 2. horse; 3. porch; 4. storm; Answers will vary.

Page 45
er: her, germ, after, letter, nerve; ir: stir, third, first, skirt, chirp, shirt, birth, girl; ur: burn, turtle, curve, purr, turn, fur, curl

Page 46
from left to right and top to bottom: 8, 14, 13, 7, 6, 1, 11, 9, 5, 4, 2, 3, 10, 12

Page 47
1. you'll; 2. we'll; 3. he'll; 4. they'll; 5. I'll; 6. she'll

Page 48
1. hasn't; 2. didn't; 3. don't; 4. haven't; 5. isn't

Page 49
1. Where + is; 2. she + is; 3. That + is; 4. what + is

Page 50
1. I + have = I've; 2. You + have = You've; 3. We + have = We've; 4. They + have = They've

Page 51
1. Let us; 2. We are; 3. You are; 4. I am; 5. They are

Page 52
1. snail; 2. trail; 3. plain; 4. day; 5. stay; 6. paint; 7. pail; 8. rain

Page 53
1. sea; 2. seals; 3. feet; 4. meal; 5. easy; 6. beach

Page 54
1. toe; 2. soap; 3. coat; 4. doe; 5. goat

Page 55
1. bread; 2. spread; 3. weather; 4. ready; 5. heavy; 6. feather; 7. head; 8. breath; a sweater

Page 56
moon: room, noon, spoon, boot, food; book: foot, cook, good, wood, hook

Page 57
1. saw; 2. yawn; 3. auto; 4. laundry; 5. hawk; 6. fawn

Page 58
ou: found, Scout, our, outside, loud, couch, house, mouse; ow: town, how, meow, Now, brown

Answer Key

Page 60
I. coins; 2. toys; 3. point; 4. oil; 5. boil;
6. boy

Page 61
I. screw; 2. stew; 3. chew; 4. dew;
5. new

Page 62
I. oo; 2. ea; 3. aw; 4. oo; 5. ea; 6. oo

Page 63
I. wanted; 2. laughed; 3. jumped;
4. marched; 5. cheered

Page 64
I. e.; 2. d.; 3. b.; 4. a.; 5. c.; 6. finding;
7. wanting; 8. playing; 9. snacking

Page 65
I. d.; 2. c.; 3. e.; 4. b.; 5. a.; 6. f.;
7. marked; 8. wishing; 9. checked;
10. breaking

Page 67
I. B.; 2. C.; 3. small, spring, lift;
4. Answers will vary.

Page 69
I. B.; 2. by, sky; it, lit; 3. B.; 4. Answers will
vary.

Page 71
I. C.; 2. B.; 3. grow, row; day, sway; cup,
up; you, too; 4. B.; 5. raindrops

Page 73
I. sight: storm clouds moving in; touch:
tiny sprinkles on my face; taste: letting
little drops inside; sound: tapping on
my window; smell: fresh air; 2. adverbs:
slowly, quietly, gently, roughly; adjectives:
beautiful, fresh; 3. B.; 4. The rain;
5. Answers will vary.

Page 75
I. C.; 2. A.; 3. A.; 4. snowman, outside,
snowball, snowballs; 5. Answers will vary.

Page 77
I. B.; 2. C.; 3. short vowel words: splash,
rock, in, sun; long vowel words: Eli, week,
sleeps, likes; 4. Answers will vary.

Page 79
I. A.; 2. short vowel words: trip, apples,
patch, pumpkin, after; long vowel words:
Lee, hay, ride; 3. hayride, applesauce,
barnyard; 4. Answers will vary.

Page 81
I. A.; 2. C.; 3. summer, sunshine, outside,
Autumn, quickly, shorten, water, before

Page 83
I. B.; 2. A.; 3. F, T, F, F; 4. Answers will vary
but can include kangaroos, opossums,
wombats, etc.

Page 85
I. D.; 2. A.; 3. A.; 4. Answers will vary.

Page 87
I. A.; 2. wild pigs, squealed; monkeys,
chattered; frogs, croaked; snakes,
hissed; 3. F, T, T, T, F, T

Page 89
I. A.; 2. B.; 3. F, T, T; 4. B.

Page 91
I. A.; 2. sing, talk; sit, stand; loud, quiet;
proud, humble; 3. C.; 4. Answers will
vary.

Page 93
I. A.; 2. B.; 3. A.; 4. Answers will vary.

Answer Key

Page 94
everywhere, sailboat, railroad, applesauce, baseball

Page 95
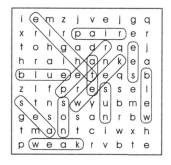

Page 96
rainbow, firefly, spiderweb, sunglasses, basketball; Answers will vary.

Page 97–99
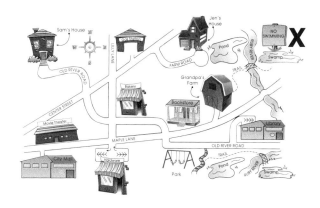

Page 100
I. Take Center Street. Turn left onto Lilly Lane. Turn left onto Maple Lane. Turn right on Old River Road. Turn left into the library lot.; 2. no; 3. yes; 4. B.

Page 101
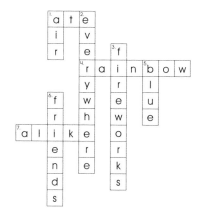

Page 102

	Cat	Dog	Gerbil	Bird
Holly	X	X	X	O
Amanda	O	X	X	X
John	X	X	O	X
Greg	X	O	X	X

Page 103
I. Greg, Holly, John, Amanda; 2. Holly, bird; Amanda, cat; John, gerbil; Greg, dog; 3. Answers will vary.

Page 104

	Square, striped with bow	Square, flowered with bow	Square, flowered without bow	Rectangle, striped with bow
Kate	O	X	X	X
Kelly	X	O	X	X
Lisa	X	X	X	O
Meg	X	X	O	X

Page 105
I. A.; 2. B.; 3. D.; 4. Answers will vary.

Page 107
I. B.; 2. A.; 3. ate, sun, blue, pair;
4. break, brake; ate, eight; sun, son; pair, pear; week, weak; blew, blue

Page 109
I. A.; 2. 3, I, 4, 2, 5; 3. B.; 4. Answers will vary.

Answer Key

Page 111
1. B.; 2. B.; 3. Nathan, Mother, sweater;
4. Answers will vary.

Page 113
1. A.; 2. parrot, gerbil, rabbit, cat, turtle,
mouse; 3. B.; 4. A.

Page 115
1. C.; 2. A.; 3. T, F, F, T, F, F; 4. sleeps,
bottle, washed, knows, playing, flowers

Page 117
1. A.; 2. A.; 3. C.; 4. Answers will vary.

Page 119
1. C.; 2. A.; 3. D.; 4. Answers will vary.

Page 121
1. B.; 2. C.; 3. B.; 4. Answers will vary.

Page 123
1.

2. B.; 3. T, T, F, F; 4. C.

Page 124
A. 1, 10, 6, 4, 9; B. 31, 13, 43, 89, 24; C. 5,
0, 11, 7, 2; D. 75, 29, 67, 18, 68; E. 3, 14, 30,
16, 50; F. 99, 15, 88, 100, 17

Page 125

0	1	2	3	4	5	6	7	8	9
10	11	12	13	14	15	16	17	18	19
20	21	22	23	24	25	26	27	28	29
30	31	32	33	34	35	36	37	38	39
40	41	42	43	44	45	46	47	48	49

A. 46; B. 10; C. 28; D. 33

Page 126

50	51	52	53	54	55	56	57	58	59
60	61	62	63	64	65	66	67	68	69
70	71	72	73	74	75	76	77	78	79
80	81	82	83	84	85	86	87	88	89
90	91	92	93	94	95	96	97	98	99

A. 52, 54, 56, 58; B. 83, 85, 87, 89; C. 66

Page 127

0	1	2	3	4	5	6	7	8	9
10	11	12	13	14	15	16	17	18	19
20	21	22	23	24	25	26	27	28	29
30	31	32	33	34	35	36	37	38	39
40	41	42	43	44	45	46	47	48	49
50	51	52	53	54	55	56	57	58	59
60	61	62	63	64	65	66	67	68	69
70	71	72	73	74	75	76	77	78	79
80	81	82	83	84	85	86	87	88	89
90	91	92	93	94	95	96	97	98	99

Page 128
A. 11, 8, 6, 15, 10; B. 9, 11, 3, 7, 14; C. 14,
18, 9, 9, 16; D. 8, 13, 1, 9, 19; E. 12, 10, 0, 4,
17

Page 129
A. 8, 5, 3, 0, 8; B. 0, 1, 7, 2, 0; C. 6, 4, 8, 2,
1; D. 6, 4, 5, 3, 3; E. 2, 7, 4, 9, 2

Answer Key

Page 130
A. 10, 6, 14, 12, 2, 5; B. 14, 13, 2, 14, 13, 11; C. 8, 12, 13, 18, 5, 5; D. 6, 19, 16, 14, 20, 12

Page 131
A. 10, 2, 5, 7, 0, 9; B. 0, 1, 9, 4, 4, 7; C. 3, 7, 1, 11, 5, 3; D. 2, 7, 4, 0, 7, 1

Page 132
A. 11, 7, 18, 8, 5; B. 19, 9, 11, 8, 5; C. 16, 0, 5, 10, 10; D. 8, 2, 10, 6, 13; E. 19, 6, 16, 10, 12

Page 133
A. 9 − 7 = 2 dogs; B. 5 − 3 = 2 rosebushes; C. 10 − 7 = 3 nuts; D. 12 − 6 = 6 crayons

Page 134
A. 12, 3, 3, 10, 1; B. 5, 4, 8, 1, 1; C. 10, 10, 3, 5, 0; D. 3, 7, 2, 0, 5; E. 3, 9, 11, 4, 3; F. 2, 4, 5, 3, 6

Page 135
A. 7, 7, 1, 5, 11; B. 9, 11, 5, 10, 2; C. 10, 11, 9, 0, 4; D. 6, 2, 2, 12, 3; E. 10, 12, 3, 12, 4; F. 6, 4, 0, 11, 10

Page 136
A. 6 + 5 = 11 miles; B. 8 − 4 = 4 bananas; C. 9 + 3 = 12 children; D. 12 − 2 = 10 boys; E. 11 − 8 = 3 cars

Page 137
A. 13, 15, 18, 14, 15; B. 17, 14, 17, 13, 13; C. 16, 17, 13, 16, 14; D. 18, 16, 18, 15, 17; E. 18, 16, 14, 13, 17; F. 18, 17, 16, 13, 15

Page 138
A. 16 − 12 = 4, 14 − 7 = 7, 18 − 17 = 1, 15 − 10 = 5, 13 − 11 = 2; B. 18 − 2 = 16, 13 − 5 = 8, 15 − 2 = 13, 16 − 6 = 10, 18 − 9 = 9; C. 17 − 4 = 13, 13 − 3 = 10, 16 − 5 = 11, 15 − 14 = 1, 18 − 0 = 18; D. 16 − 16 = 0, 15 − 1 = 14, 17 − 5 = 12, 18 − 11 = 7, 13 − 0 = 13;

E. 14 − 13 = 1, 13 − 4 = 9, 16 − 9 = 7, 15 − 3 = 12, 17 − 9 = 8; F. 18 − 13 = 5, 13 − 6 = 7, 16 − 4 = 12, 14 − 6 = 8, 15 − 11 = 4

Page 139
A. 9, 10, 15, 15, 16; B. 13, 14, 9, 14, 9; C. 6, 18, 15, 13, 5; D. 14, 8, 16, 7, 9; E. 18, 3, 17, 6, 15; F. 13, 4, 5, 18, 6

Page 140

100	101	102	103	104	105	106	107	108	109
110	111	112	113	114	115	116	117	118	119
120	121	122	123	124	125	126	127	128	129
130	131	132	133	134	135	136	137	138	139
140	141	142	143	144	145	146	147	148	149

Page 141

150	151	152	153	154	155	156	157	158	159
160	161	162	163	164	165	166	167	168	169
170	171	172	173	174	175	176	177	178	179
180	181	182	183	184	185	186	187	188	189
190	191	192	193	194	195	196	197	198	199

Page 142

100	101	102	103	104	105	106	107	108	109
110	111	112	113	114	115	116	117	118	119
120	121	122	123	124	125	126	127	128	129
130	131	132	133	134	135	136	137	138	139
140	141	142	143	144	145	146	147	148	149
150	151	152	153	154	155	156	157	158	159
160	161	162	163	164	165	166	167	168	169
170	171	172	173	174	175	176	177	178	179
180	181	182	183	184	185	186	187	188	189
190	191	192	193	194	195	196	197	198	199

Answer Key

Page 143

A. 19, 15, 27, 19, 27; B. 19, 16, 19, 17, 24;
C. 28, 19, 14, 18, 28; D. 23, 27, 19, 26, 17;
E. 28, 29, 15, 19, 16

Page 144

A. 7, 6, 12, 0, 11; B. 3, 14, 0, 4, 13; C. 17, 6,
11, 7, 16; D. 7, 9, 4, 2, 16

Page 145

A. 8 + 2 = 10, 3 + 5 = 8, 5 + 2 = 7,
5 + 7 = 12, 8 + 9 = 17; B. 8 + 10 = 18, 3 + 1
= 4, 7 + 7 = 14, 5 + 11 = 16, 6 + 3 = 9; C. 1
+ 3 = 4, 6 + 4 = 10, 1 + 8 = 9, 1 + 14 = 15,
3 + 13 = 16; D. 7 + 2 = 9, 3 + 5 = 8, 8 + 6 =
14, 6 + 7 = 13, 1 + 4 = 5; E. 6 + 6 = 12, 5 +
1 = 6, 7 + 6 = 13, 7 + 0 = 7, 0 + 0 = 0; F. 2 +
3 = 5, 2 + 6 = 8, 3 + 4 = 7, 2 + 2 = 4, 10 + 2
= 12

Page 146

A. 6 − 2 = 4, 11 − 6 = 5, 8 − 7 = 1,
5 − 2 = 3, 3 − 1 = 2; B. 14 − 13 = 1,
13 − 4 = 9, 16 − 9 = 7, 15 − 3 = 12,
17 − 9 = 8; C. 18 − 3 = 15, 15 − 7 = 8,
14 − 4 = 10, 13 − 12 = 1, 16 − 8 = 8;
D. 16 − 1 = 15, 13 − 8 = 5, 16 − 15 = 1,
18 − 6 = 12, 17 − 7 = 10; E. 17 − 4 = 13, 13 −
3 = 10, 16 − 5 = 11, 15 − 14 = 1, 18 − 0 = 18;
F. 16 − 11 = 5, 14 − 13 = 1, 18 − 8 = 10, 17 −
8 = 9, 14 − 1 = 13

Page 147

A. 17, 19, 25, 17, 17; B. 16, 29, 19, 19, 15;
C. 29, 23, 17, 18, 19; D. 19, 28, 16, 14, 17;
E. 16, 19, 16, 17, 17

Page 148

A. 6, 18, 7, 1, 5; B. 14, 8, 0, 7, 9; C. 10, 3, 2,
6, 3; D. 7, 0, 15, 9, 16; E. 12, 5, 10, 10, 9;
F. 5, 8, 6, 8, 9

Page 149

A. 12:00 − 9:00 = 3 hours; B. 3:00 − 1:00 =
2 hours; C. 19 − 8 = 11 students; D. 12 − 9
= 3 pages

Page 150

200	201	202	203	204	205	206	207	208	209
210	211	212	213	214	215	216	217	218	219
220	221	222	223	224	225	226	227	228	229
230	231	232	233	234	235	236	237	238	239
240	241	242	243	244	245	246	247	248	249

Page 151

250	251	252	253	254	255	256	257	258	259
260	261	262	263	264	265	266	267	268	269
270	271	272	273	274	275	276	277	278	279
280	281	282	283	284	285	286	287	288	289
290	291	292	293	294	295	296	297	298	299

Page 152

200	201	202	203	204	205	206	207	208	209
210	211	212	213	214	215	216	217	218	219
220	221	222	223	224	225	226	227	228	229
230	231	232	233	234	235	236	237	238	239
240	241	242	243	244	245	246	247	248	249
250	251	252	253	254	255	256	257	258	259
260	261	262	263	264	265	266	267	268	269
270	271	272	273	274	275	276	277	278	279
280	281	282	283	284	285	286	287	288	289
290	291	292	293	294	295	296	297	298	299

Page 153

A. 3:00; B. 6:00; C. 7:30; D. 12:00;
E. 12:30; F. 9:30; G. 11:00; H. 8:30

Page 154

A. 5; B. 60; C. 12; D. 30; E. 15; F. 35;
G. 45; H. 1; I. 12; J. 24

Answer Key

Page 155
A. 2:15; B. 8:10; C. 10:35; D. 9:45; E. 1:35;
F. 3:10; G. 10:30; H. 5:50

Page 156
A. 10:10, 10, 10; B. 1:50, 50, 1; C. 1:25, 25,
1; D. 3:15, 15, 3; E. 6:45, 45, 6; F. 4:40, 40, 4

Page 157
A. 11:00 – 8:00 = 3 hours; B. 3:20 – 1:20 = 2
hours; C. 4:30 – 4:00 = 30 minutes;
D. 10:55 – 10:35 = 20 minutes; E. 6:30

Page 158

300	301	302	303	304	305	306	307	308	309
310	311	312	313	314	315	316	317	318	319
320	321	322	323	324	325	326	327	328	329
330	331	332	333	334	335	336	337	338	339
340	341	342	343	344	345	346	347	348	349

Page 159

350	351	352	353	354	355	356	357	358	359
360	361	362	363	364	365	366	367	368	369
370	371	372	373	374	375	376	377	378	379
380	381	382	383	384	385	386	387	388	389
390	391	392	393	394	395	396	397	398	399

Page 160

300	301	302	303	304	305	306	307	308	309
310	311	312	313	314	315	316	317	318	319
320	321	322	323	324	325	326	327	328	329
330	331	332	333	334	335	336	337	338	339
340	341	342	343	344	345	346	347	348	349
350	351	352	353	354	355	356	357	358	359
360	361	362	363	364	365	366	367	368	369
370	371	372	373	374	375	376	377	378	379
380	381	382	383	384	385	386	387	388	389
390	391	392	393	394	395	396	397	398	399

Page 161
A. 12, 14, 7, 12, 18; B. 12, 18, 12, 16, 16;
C. 18, 20, 16, 20, 18; D. 14, 23, 19, 19, 19

Page 162
A. 35, 28, 53, 39, 39; B. 29, 56, 96, 75, 85;
C. 69, 66, 97, 26, 39; D. 28, 39, 94, 35, 92;
E. 35, 44, 35, 38, 47; F. 55, 56, 47, 63, 24

Page 163
A. 6, 16, 50, 23, 44; B. 3, 51, 13, 40, 22;
C. 1, 10, 52, 51, 16; D. 12, 20, 2, 5, 31;
E. 40, 3, 15, 72, 45; F. 64, 30, 11, 63, 21

Page 164
A. 64, 57, 96, 29, 42; B. 40, 97, 90, 54, 22;
C. 29, 13, 99, 31, 69; D. 21, 20, 10, 39, 11;
E. 23, 34, 36, 99, 21; F. 2, 99, 44, 40, 27

Page 165
A. 10, 40, 51, 31, 55; B. 14, 20, 23, 13, 10;
C. 6, 16, 50, 23, 44; D. 10, 44, 64, 22, 50;
E. 22, 40, 83, 32, 55

Page 166
A. 89, 57, 86, 49, 76; B. 40, 78, 80, 66, 96;
C. 37, 56, 98, 79, 69; D. 99, 90, 30, 79, 93;
E. 68, 98, 75, 98, 89

Page 167
A. 3, 51, 13, 40, 22; B. 1, 10, 52, 51, 16;
C. 12, 20, 2, 5, 31; D. 40, 1, 15, 72, 45;
E. 30, 11, 63, 21, 8

Page 168

400	401	402	403	404	405	406	407	408	409
410	411	412	413	414	415	416	417	418	419
420	421	422	423	424	425	426	427	428	429
430	431	432	433	434	435	436	437	438	439
440	441	442	443	444	445	446	447	448	449

Answer Key

Page 169

450	451	452	453	454	455	456	457	458	459
460	461	462	463	464	465	466	467	468	469
470	471	472	473	474	475	476	477	478	479
480	481	482	483	484	485	486	487	488	489
490	491	492	493	494	495	496	497	498	499

Page 170

400	401	402	403	404	405	406	407	408	409
410	411	412	413	414	415	416	417	418	419
420	421	422	423	424	425	426	427	428	429
430	431	432	433	434	435	436	437	438	439
440	441	442	443	444	445	446	447	448	449
450	451	452	453	454	455	456	457	458	459
460	461	462	463	464	465	466	467	468	469
470	471	472	473	474	475	476	477	478	479
480	481	482	483	484	485	486	487	488	489
490	491	492	493	494	495	496	497	498	499

Page 171
A. 8, 3, 83; B. 4, 1, 41; C. 3, 7, 37; D. 9, 4, 94; E. 6, 5, 65; F. 1, 4, 14; G. 7, 8, 78; H. 7, 0, 70

Page 172
A. 3, 3, 2, 332; B. 4, 0, 5, 405; C. 9, 3, 0, 930

Page 173
A. 2, 3, 4, 234; B. 1, 0, 9, 109; C. 4, 4, 4, 444; D. 2, 3, 2, 232

Page 174
A. 726, 963, 976, 825, 927; B. 500, 677, 253, 575, 368; C. 973, 999, 697, 666, 358; D. 969, 478, 758, 863, 900; E. 797, 788, 797, 776, 252; F. 977, 758, 798, 308, 525

Page 175
A. 741, 153, 507, 584, 624; B. 375, 130, 238, 710, 50; C. 114, 521, 321, 114, 550; D. 450, 212, 521, 242, 630; E. 121, 343, 111, 301, 747; F. 430, 412, 121, 200, 164

Page 176
A. 324 + 271 = 595; B. 656 − 223 = 433; C. 326 − 214 = 112; D. 845 − 325 = 520

Page 177
A. 369, 989, 385, 527, 987; B. 898, 913; 999, 409, 566; C. 489, 582, 749, 388, 851; D. 788, 893, 793, 488, 379

Page 178
A. 341, 203, 212, 216, 102; B. 555, 17, 121, 220, 10; C. 114, 231, 114, 412, 532; D. 251, 684, 403, 242, 203; E. 400, 511, 218, 215, 312

Page 179
A. 452 − 241 = 211; B. 567 − 325 = 242; C. 286 − 160 = 126; D. 724 − 510 = 214

Page 180

500	501	502	503	504	505	506	507	508	509
510	511	512	513	514	515	516	517	518	519
520	521	522	523	524	525	526	527	528	529
530	531	532	533	534	535	536	537	538	539
540	541	542	543	544	545	546	547	548	549

Page 181

550	551	552	553	554	555	556	557	558	559
560	561	562	563	564	565	566	567	568	569
570	571	572	573	574	575	576	577	578	579
580	581	582	583	584	585	586	587	588	589
590	591	592	593	594	595	596	597	598	599

Answer Key

Page 182

500	501	502	503	504	505	506	507	508	509
510	511	512	513	514	515	516	517	518	519
520	521	522	523	524	525	526	527	528	529
530	531	532	533	534	535	536	537	538	539
540	541	542	543	544	545	546	547	548	549
550	551	552	553	554	555	556	557	558	559
560	561	562	563	564	565	566	567	568	569
570	571	572	573	574	575	576	577	578	579
580	581	582	583	584	585	586	587	588	589
590	591	592	593	594	595	596	597	598	599

Page 183

A. 75¢; B. 50¢; C. 35¢; D. 35¢; E. 52¢

Page 184

A. 60¢, no; B. 50¢, yes; C. 95¢, yes;
D. 29¢, no; E. 80¢, no

Page 185

A. 49¢, no; B. 100¢, yes; C. 58¢, no;
D. 57¢, yes; E. 50¢, yes

Page 186

A. 54¢; B. 75¢; C. 65¢; D. 13¢

Page 187

A. 60¢; B. 100¢; C. 44¢; D. 59¢

Page 188

600	601	602	603	604	605	606	607	608	609
610	611	612	613	614	615	616	617	618	619
620	621	622	623	624	625	626	627	628	629
630	631	632	633	634	635	636	637	638	639
640	641	642	643	644	645	646	647	648	649

Page 189

650	651	652	653	654	655	656	657	658	659
660	661	662	663	664	665	666	667	668	669
670	671	672	673	674	675	676	677	678	679
680	681	682	683	684	685	686	687	688	689
690	691	692	693	694	695	696	697	698	699

Page 190

600	601	602	603	604	605	606	607	608	609
610	611	612	613	614	615	616	617	618	619
620	621	622	623	624	625	626	627	628	629
630	631	632	633	634	635	636	637	638	639
640	641	642	643	644	645	646	647	648	649
650	651	652	653	654	655	656	657	658	659
660	661	662	663	664	665	666	667	668	669
670	671	672	673	674	675	676	677	678	679
680	681	682	683	684	685	686	687	688	689
690	691	692	693	694	695	696	697	698	699

Page 191

A. $\frac{1}{4}$; B. $\frac{3}{8}$; C. $\frac{2}{4}$; D. $\frac{1}{3}$

Page 192

A. $\frac{1}{4}$; B. $\frac{1}{2}$; C. $\frac{1}{8}$; D. $\frac{2}{3}$; E. $\frac{4}{5}$;

F. $\frac{6}{10}$

Page 193

700	701	702	703	704	705	706	707	708	709
710	711	712	713	714	715	716	717	718	719
720	721	722	723	724	725	726	727	728	729
730	731	732	733	734	735	736	737	738	739
740	741	742	743	744	745	746	747	748	749

Answer Key

Page 194

750	751	752	753	754	755	756	757	758	759
760	761	762	763	764	765	766	767	768	769
770	771	772	773	774	775	776	777	778	779
780	781	782	783	784	785	786	787	788	789
790	791	792	793	794	795	796	797	798	799

Page 195

700	701	702	703	704	705	706	707	708	709
710	711	712	713	714	715	716	717	718	719
720	721	722	723	724	725	726	727	728	729
730	731	732	733	734	735	736	737	738	739
740	741	742	743	744	745	746	747	748	749
750	751	752	753	754	755	756	757	758	759
760	761	762	763	764	765	766	767	768	769
770	771	772	773	774	775	776	777	778	779
780	781	782	783	784	785	786	787	788	789
790	791	792	793	794	795	796	797	798	799

Page 196
A. 86, 70, 81, 63, 36; B. 62, 41, 60, 92, 33; C. 96, 94, 93, 33, 85; D. 42, 80, 51, 101, 100

Page 197
A. 42, 92, 86, 50, 57; B. 50, 151, 82, 95, 136; C. 93, 37, 106, 121, 100; D. 111, 143, 134, 121, 104; E. 90, 52, 70, 71, 103; F. 123, 70, 130, 130, 113

Page 198
A. 53, 47, 85, 77, 111; B. 111, 82, 96, 48, 51; C. 93, 77, 32, 51, 71; D. 138, 87, 89, 115, 114; E. 82, 55, 66, 107, 109

Page 199
A. 91, 63, 65, 86, 49; B. 76, 74, 106, 145, 80; C. 87, 45, 118, 109, 48; D. 85, 116, 125, 52, 76; E. 44, 89, 79, 69, 31

Page 200
A. 76, 45, 35, 102, 89; B. 122, 94, 66, 84, 139; C. 39, 97, 49, 85, 40; D. 102, 134, 113, 78, 36; E. 70, 94, 98, 65, 39

Page 201
A. 73, 89, 92, 69, 39, 84; B. 27, 115, 39, 73, 87, 37; C. 108, 94, 140, 134, 62, 132; D. 112, 73, 51, 129, 79, 109

Page 202
Across: 1. 117; 2. 16; 4. 108; 5. 100; 6. 70; 7. 1,047; 9. 13; 10. 57; 11. 45; 12. 598; 13. 86; 15. 100; Down: 1. 115; 2. 128; 3. 120; 4. 12; 7. 13; 8. 284; 12. 531; 13. 86; 14. 13

Page 203

Page 204
A. 81, 132, 107, 212, 52; B. 105, 111, 40, 93, 83; C. 74, 43, 146, 94, 81; D. 103, 143, 144, 184, 184; E. 103, 54, 90, 25, 157

Page 205
A. 28 + 16 = 44 people; B. 88 + 19 = 107 bulbs; C. 24 + 69 = 93 peanuts; D. 49 + 25 = 74 cents; E. 47 + 15 = 62 CDs

Page 206
A. 374, 716, 535, 492, 990; B. 839, 685, 454, 365, 953; C. 530, 902, 566, 591, 836; D. 694, 265, 871, 683, 639; E. 762, 715, 448, 318, 539

Answer Key

Page 207
A. $3.30, $4.98, $3.27, $1.88, $1.73;
B. $5.87, $3.89, $8.59, $4.06, $9.38;
C. $7.56, $4.04, $5.95, $4.70, $7.67;
D. $3.53, $7.99, $9.90, $4.91, $2.68

Page 208
A. 1,281; 298; 1,170; 900; 423; B. 1,280;
1,032; 1,037; 556; 766; C. 278; 510; 943;
407; 478; D. 432; 668; 660; 289; 355;
E. 355; 1,309; 981; 535; 591

Page 209

800	801	802	803	804	805	806	807	808	809
810	811	812	813	814	815	816	817	818	819
820	821	822	823	824	825	826	827	828	829
830	831	832	833	834	835	836	837	838	839
840	841	842	843	844	845	846	847	848	849

Page 210

850	851	852	853	854	855	856	857	858	859
860	861	862	863	864	865	866	867	868	869
870	871	872	873	874	875	876	877	878	879
880	881	882	883	884	885	886	887	888	889
890	891	892	893	894	895	896	897	898	899

Page 211

800	801	802	803	804	805	806	807	808	809
810	811	812	813	814	815	816	817	818	819
820	821	822	823	824	825	826	827	828	829
830	831	832	833	834	835	836	837	838	839
840	841	842	843	844	845	846	847	848	849
850	851	852	853	854	855	856	857	858	859
860	861	862	863	864	865	866	867	868	869
870	871	872	873	874	875	876	877	878	879
880	881	882	883	884	885	886	887	888	889
890	891	892	893	894	895	896	897	898	899

Page 212
A. 33, 48, 53, 69, 16; B. 28, 23, 54, 39, 18;
C. 19, 19, 17, 29, 57; D. 59, 46, 38, 12, 17;
E. 18, 32, 9, 14, 65

Page 213

Page 214
A. 36, 27, 36, 36, 36; B. 19, 19, 19, 19, 58;
C. 12, 3, 12, 11, 12; D. 35, 13, 32, 17, 4;
E. 52, 10, 52, 11, 65

Page 215
A. 68, 45, 29, 17, 14; B. 48, 5, 14, 11, 14;
C. 26, 39, 46, 64, 62; D. 37, 7, 49, 9, 14; E. 9,
19, 59, 66, 32

Page 216
A. 16, 13, 26, 16, 21; B. 12, 11, 14, 45, 33;
C. 8, 3, 50, 39, 3; D. 18, 8, 10, 28, 69; E. 16,
10, 18, 59, 36

Page 217
A. 12, 12, 4, 3, 12, 11; B. 26, 26, 18, 1, 26,
26; C. 38, 12, 17, 17, 58, 17; D. 25, 21, 30, 2,
30, 30

254

© Rainbow Bridge Publishing

Answer Key

Page 218
A. 42 – 14 = 28 cans
B. 67 – 41 = 26 animal crackers
C. 52 – 14 = 38 dominoes
D. 21 – 18 = 3 days

Page 219
A. 84 – 68 = 16 peaches
B. 97 – 48 = 49 jelly beans
C. 78 – 29 = 49 bottle caps
D. 86 – 19 = 67 children

Page 220
A. 92 – 25 = 67 deer
B. 76 – 59 = 17 apples
C. 42 – 16 = 26 buttons
D. 81 + 18 = 99 rocks
E. 31 – 13 = 18 children

Page 221
A. 489, 149, 290, 199, 297; B. 187, 842, 175, 182, 519; C. 394, 308, 398, 209, 575; D. 278, 802, 625, 491, 408; E. 107, 109, 232, 793, 159

Page 222
A. 139, 277, 110, 193, 599; B. 11, 80, 286, 312, 99; C. 105, 49, 588, 403, 201; D. 100, 255, 155, 2, 198; E. 234, 83, 200, 13, 494

Page 223

900	901	902	903	904	905	906	907	908	909
910	911	912	913	914	915	916	917	918	919
920	921	922	923	924	925	926	927	928	929
930	931	932	933	934	935	936	937	938	939
940	941	942	943	944	945	946	947	948	949

Page 224

950	951	952	953	954	955	956	957	958	959
960	961	962	963	964	965	966	967	968	969
970	971	972	973	974	975	976	977	978	979
980	981	982	983	984	985	986	987	988	989
990	991	992	993	994	995	996	997	998	999

Page 225

900	901	902	903	904	905	906	907	908	909
910	911	912	913	914	915	916	917	918	919
920	921	922	923	924	925	926	927	928	929
930	931	932	933	934	935	936	937	938	939
940	941	942	943	944	945	946	947	948	949
950	951	952	953	954	955	956	957	958	959
960	961	962	963	964	965	966	967	968	969
970	971	972	973	974	975	976	977	978	979
980	981	982	983	984	985	986	987	988	989
990	991	992	993	994	995	996	997	998	999

Page 226
A. 12:30, 30, 12; B. 9:45, 45, 9;
C. 3:15, 15, 3; D. 8:10, 10, 8;
E. 12:10, 2:10, 4:10, 6:10

Page 227
A. +; B. +; C. +; D. +; E. –; F. +; G. –; H. –;

I. J, O, Y; J. ☺ ☺ ☺ ☹ ☹ ;
K. 8, 6, 2, 4, 9

Page 228
Top: 60; Middle: 96; Bottom: 11

Page 229
Top: 60; Middle: 96; Bottom: 11; Austin

Page 230
A. 4; B. 3

Answer Key

Page 231

A. 2; B. 8

Page 232

Completed picture shows a teepee.

Page 233

Lisa: $3.00; Dianne: $2.50; Mike: $2.00; Lisa had the most money left.; One puppy and one kitten should be circled.

Page 234

A. 8:15, 15, 8; B. 1:40, 40, 1; C. 11:20, 20, 11; D. 1:15, 15, 1

Page 235

92 – 16 = 76 – 27 = 49 – 15 = 34 – 4 = 30 – 15 = 15; The peanut with the number 15 should be circled.

Page 236

A. <, <, >, <; B. >, >, <, >; white; I would have more white marbles because there are more white marbles than black marbles in the bag.

Page 237

A. 42; B. 5; C. 22; D. 9; E. 60; F. 46; G. 0; H. 80; I. 34; J. 14; B. and D. should be circled.

Page 238

Across: 1. three; 4. school; 6. subtraction; 9. equation; 10. nine; 11. solve;
Down: 1. two; 2. eleven; 3. sixteen; 5. clock; 7. number; 8. hands

Page 239

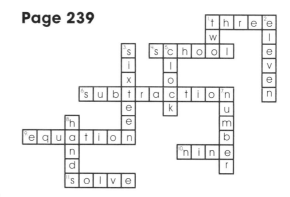

Page 240

Marcus made $10.00.

Page 241

Answers from left to right and top to bottom: 674, 923, 960, 575, 492, 363, 888, 580, 767, 590, 644; A BIRTHDAY CAKE!